Praise for Dolores Howell's
Stand Straight and Grow Tall

"Dolores Howell is an inspiration to those who are illiterate, because she was in that place. She has put her experiences into, *Stand Straight and Grow Tall,* a book that tells of her struggles to overcome the taunts of kids and the humiliation by teachers, when in truth, she had learning disabilities that were holding her back." --- *Editorial in* The Frederick News Post*, Frederick, MD*

"Your story is courageous and humbling and encouraging to those that deal with dyslexia and illiteracy." --- *Preston County Literacy Council, Morgantown WV*

"Your book, *Stand Straight and Grow Tall*...is worth every penny and more to read about all of your pain and successes. Reading your book has helped me understand how tiring and hard it is for people with learning disabilities to do a lot of reading and writing.

"As a retired kindergarten teacher, it was enlightening to read about the difficulty you had before you found out what your disability was. It is very hard to be positive and cheerful when you don't have confidence in yourself.

"It is important, I think, for people who are teachers now to read your story.

"Anyone that will read your book and share in your personal struggles will be blessed. I love your book, Dory. Bravo for all your effort and endurance. It is a beautiful story of love, faith, loyalty, hope and success. You have changed the lives of many people – some you will never know." --- *Excerpts of a letter to Dory from Linda New, Retired Teacher, Montgomery County, MD.*

STAND STRAIGHT AND GROW TALL

Revised Edition

Dolores Howell

iv

Do you no it is like to not to be abu to read to afrid that soone one will fid out? Do you what people thinck of a pirson who can not read have you every been not abu to read or spell what in font of you have you every been in a grope like bidu stdy afrid soone one will call on you to read. But sill want to lern oh so badly do you no what it is like to tavel in any sange plse an not no how read an do your shoping by looks of a box and cans. did you every go to a restrest and orer what your frand orer even if you don't like it because you can not read the menu this is why I have writen this book to tell you how unfir and unnecsary it is to send a pirson to school for years and thay come out not no how to read and spell enoth to suv.

Dedicated to my Lord Jesus,
with whom I have fought and
yelled at all the way through.

STAND STRAIGHT AND GROW TALL

Revised Edition

By

Dolores Howell

Home Crafted Artistry & Printing
New Albany, Indiana

This publication is a work of non-fiction taken from the author's life experiences, with the intention to increase awareness of very real problems still existing in society. The statements, perceptions and opinions recounted are those of the author, from the author's point of view, and have been recounted as accurately as possible. The author intends no offense to anyone, but only to bring about a greater understanding of the problems illiteracy causes. Her hopes are that by sharing her genuine experiences, fewer others will suffer.

ISBN 13: 978-1-7323437-0-2

Home Crafted Artistry & Printing
1252 Beechwood Avenue
New Albany, IN 47150
Email HomeCraftedArtistry@yahoo.com

Cover design by Mary Dow Bibb Smith

Proudly printed in the United States of America.

Table of Contents

Chapter 1   *Didn't See the Trouble Coming*   3
Chapter 2   *School Starts and So Does Trouble*   8
Chapter 3   *Junior High and High Schools* .   17
Chapter 4   *Evading Discovery*   .   .   27
Chapter 5   *To Tell the Truth* .   .   .   36
Chapter 6   *A Break Though at Last*   .   53
Chapter 7   *Schools and Psychologists*   .   65
Chapter 8   *Music*   80
Chapter 9   *Here We Go Again.*   .   .   89
Chapter 10   *The Seventh Day Adventist School*   99
Chapter 11   *Tutoring*   113
Chapter 12   *The Last of Schooling?* .   .   125
Chapter 13   *Retired to Antique Dealing*   .   131
Chapter 14   *The Importance of This Book* .   141

Three Selections of Poetry and Prose of Dolores Howell
Unteachable   149
My Tutor   151
Life of an Apple   152

STAND STRAIGHT
AND GROW TALL

Chapter 1
Didn't See the Trouble Coming

Looking back over my early years on the farm in West Virginia, it is the one room schoolhouse, built on land donated by my mother's family, which remains in my mind. The schoolhouse, which was also a church on weekends, point to two areas of my life, school and church, which have never let me alone, much as I wanted to escape them both.

In those early years, nothing gave me or my family a hint of the trouble which has haunted me so much of my life. The clues, which might give evidence to a professional person now, went unnoticed then. My parents didn't look for trouble; they had enough of it anyway.

I was born in 1936, the seventh of eight children. Times were very hard in those depression years. We lived on my mother's family's 80-acre farm in an isolated community in West Virginia. When my father was home, which wasn't often, he would work on the farm, which consisted of a cornfield, a garden and an orchard. Often my father found work in other cities, and Mother and the older children took care of the garden. My family's diet was mostly fresh vegetables and fruit in the summer, milk from our two cows, and canned vegetables and fruit in the winter. When Daddy came home, he brought food, which usually lasted our large family only a few days.

During the winter, when snowdrifts blocked the 3-mile lane winding through those steep hills to our house, even walking was almost impossible, and we often ran out of food. Mother would see that her children were fed, and then she would eat the leftovers. Because of this, she ate very little, even during her pregnancy with me. She was probably hungry most of the time, but she never complained. It has made me wonder in later years if lack of proper food contributed to my problems with learning.

Many of the people who lived in that area were moving to find jobs in other places, but Mother loved the farm she was born and raised on, and never wanted to leave it. The white, two-story house had three bedrooms, a kitchen, living room, dining room and parlor. The smell of wood burning in the cook stove in the kitchen was always present.

Sometimes on warm evenings, we would sit on the back porch swing and talk. The only sounds that filled the quiet were crickets, the train in the distance, and sometimes a wildcat scream. And always there was the sound of the creek running close by. Downstream a short distance was the schoolhouse.

Education was not as important in the hills of West Virginia as it was in the cities, but it was important in Mother's family. Her mother, grandmother, two sisters and a brother were schoolteachers. Their training, typical of the time,

4

was eight years in public school and two years in Normal School. Mother's brother was 16 years old the first year he taught school. He was principal of an elementary school for many years.

Like my mother, he had a good sense of humor. One Sunday while my uncle was attending church, the minister, with a voice like an auctioneer, was preaching. He proclaimed firmly, "It says right here, in Pizlamus IV, uh…"

My uncle, realizing he meant Psalms IV, burst out laughing. The next Sunday the sermon was about my uncle.

Mother was able to laugh, too, and we heard funny stories about her experiences in nursing. She was a registered nurse, and never hesitated to help others when she was needed, even though taking care of her own family took nearly all her time and effort.

Even with all the problems we children caused her, and there were many serious accidents and illnesses, Mother found time to read whenever she had a newspaper. My earliest memories of Mother are of her reading children's books to us at bedtime by the light of the oil lamp.

My father read often, too, and liked reading aloud to the family and visitors. His personality, though, was just the opposite of Mother's. I remember him as a free spirit, sometimes impulsive and quick-tempered. He was a heavy drinker who sought and enjoyed the companionship of other women.

When Daddy got a job with the Baltimore and Ohio Railroad, our family moved from the farm to a six-room duplex in Cumberland, Maryland. I was five years old. Cumberland seemed a lot different from the quiet, lonely farm. It must have been very hard for Mother.

For us kids, it meant more children to play with. We were the largest family on the street, but now we had children other than brothers and sisters to play with. Out of all those kids there was only one girl my age, Anna Saylor. Anna became my best friend and her parents treated me like a member of the family.

The fact that I was a real tomboy didn't seem to bother the Saylors. Maybe they thought it was because I had so many brothers or had run wild in the hills of West Virginia. Anna and I played with dolls, cutouts and coloring books, if it was too cold to be outside. I knew that Anna's coloring was better than mine was. Mrs. Saylor, who seemed to like me very much, would look at Anna's coloring and tell her how good it was. Then she would look at mine and kindly say, "Yours is good, too, Dory, but try to stay in the lines. The sky and the girl's eyes are blue, but her face isn't."

When I could, though, I would be outside, climbing a tree or playing games with the boys. My brothers also collected comic books, and I enjoyed looking at the pictures, but could never make the words out. Mother, though she loved to read and valued education, was too busy and too worn out to notice that my coloring was sloppy, or that, even as I was ready to start first grade, I wasn't trying to learn to read, or print my name.

At Anna's birthday party in June, Mrs. Saylor said that Anna and I would be going to school together in September. I didn't think about it again until a week before school started, when Anna got new school clothes. I wondered if I was going to get new clothes too, and even though I didn't, I remember looking forward to school with the same joy as all the other kids.

Chapter 2
School Starts and So Does Trouble

The morning when I went to school for the first time, I was excited like the other kids. It's probably good I had no idea of the suffering and pain I would go through during my school years. It didn't take long to overwhelm me. I failed the first grade, but I had no idea why. I couldn't understand why Anna and some of my classmates were going to the second grade and I wasn't.

When I got to school on the first day of my second year, I didn't know what classroom to go into. I went to the room where some of my former classmates were and I was told I was in the wrong room. I got upset, began to cry, and ran home. My father was there. He got angry that I had come home and made me return to school. I did.

On my return, the teacher came over and tried to comfort me by telling me I was in the right room. As I looked around, I saw that I was back in the room where I had been the year before, but with a different teacher and different children except for the few boys who were also repeating first grade.

Mother read my report cards without any comments. No one in the family ever scolded me or punished me for not doing well in school. Maybe they could tell how badly I felt. I wanted to learn to read. I didn't care about math or spelling. I just wanted to be able to stand up and read.

No one in my family knew that I couldn't read, not even Mother. I went to school. Everyone who went to school learns how to read. We all believed that. Mother was so overwhelmed with problems she didn't have time to sit down and ask, "How was school?" I don't know what I would have said if she had asked, for very early I learned not being able to read was bad. I was embarrassed when my classmates would tell me that I was so dumb I didn't know how to spell "cat". I knew it was true.

Failing first grade was confusing. Failing second grade was heartbreaking. At the time, I began to withdraw. Those around me learned the alphabet, how to read, how to print. I didn't learn. I could print my name, but even my drawings and paintings were very poor. When I learned anything, it was because of a great deal of repetition, as in learning rhymes for jumping rope. In the classroom itself, I wasn't even learning to count, much less add or subtract.

"Pay attention," were the words I heard most often from the teacher. I was never a discipline problem because I didn't want to get whacked with a ruler or slapped on the face. The embarrassment would have hurt more than the physical pain, so I behaved myself.

There was a high point the year I went to third grade, but it didn't happen in school. One of our neighbors had a son my age. The family attended a storefront church that held a contest for memorizing Bible verses. Each child who memorized a certain number of Bible verses won a Bible. My brother Jimmy and I thought this was a great challenge. It certainly was to me. We worked very hard on the verses and Mother helped by giving us the words.

Jimmy won his Bible weeks before I did. By that time I was used to others being ahead of me and I kept on struggling to memorize five verses. Finally I did. Winning that Bible was like getting a treasure for me.

Whether I passed a grade or failed it, I felt like a failure. I wasn't learning and I didn't know why. The pressure was building inside of me. The boys I had been with since first grade teased me every chance they got. By fourth grade, I was still the only girl in this lowest reading group. The teacher, too, often said unkind things to me in front of the class: "Dolores, why can't you do your work?" "Why don't you try to do better?" "Why do you just sit there?" "Why don't you pay attention?"

One time I chewed the top of the pencil and she handed the pencil to me in front of the whole class and made me use it. She had taught my three brothers before me and was always saying they were not as lazy as I was. No one said directly that there was something wrong with me, but I knew there was and I blamed myself completely.

I couldn't understand why the kids didn't like me. One of the girls was giving a birthday party and invited every girl in the class but me. One of those invited asked her in front of me why I hadn't been invited. She answered that her mother didn't have enough plates.

The year my reading group, those same four boys and me, was passed from the fourth grade to the sixth I felt better about myself. I had done something the smarter kids had not done. I didn't realize then that the school officials didn't know what else to do with us. My math and reading had not improved, and might never improve, and there was no one to help.

Summers were usually a welcome relief, but the summer before I was to go to sixth grade I had an unhappy experience, which stuck with me long into adulthood.

Each summer, after we had moved from West Virginia, Mother would take us four younger children back to the farm to visit. There were only two other families with children; most people had left to find jobs elsewhere. Even though it was lonely, it was such a welcome change to be away from school that I didn't mind. Before we left for the farm on this summer, I went to Sunday School with Anna, as I sometimes did. On this Sunday, I was asked to read the lesson. I just sat there looking at the book. It was such a surprise that my usual defenses failed me.

Finally, kindly, Anna said, "She can't read." I wanted the earth to swallow me.

By the end of the summer in West Virginia, the incident had faded a little from my mind. The first day of school, going into the sixth grade, a girl who had been at Sunday School that day pointed me out to a group of other girls. "See that girl over there," she said so I could hear, "She can't read." They all laughed. I wanted to run, but there was no place to go.

I never went back to that Sunday School again.

Even with that bad start, though, my sixth grade was happier because I had a kind teacher who tried to help me. I was still not learning much, but I could tell the teacher liked me and this made all the difference. While I was in Miss Carter's class, I didn't feel pressured. She was firm, but never mean. Although she didn't understand why I wasn't learning any more than the other teachers had, she surely did try to help. That year even the kids liked me.

This added support made me feel better, but it didn't help my learning. In reading, I began to guess and grab at words. Sometimes I was right, but more often wrong. When I was wrong, I didn't even know it. I began to change a sentence or sometimes a whole page, to fit the word I thought I saw. Often these were words that looked alike, such as ball/bell or left/felt. On top of that, I couldn't distinguish between the short vowel sounds. I would say words the way I thought I heard them, which was very often wrong.

Teachers may have thought it was a West Virginia dialect; no one tried to find out why I mispronounced words. Dealing with any small symbols, numbers or individual letters has always been hard for me.

Any paper I wrote was poor at the beginning but poorer at the end. The cursive I had managed to learn was not much help in putting what was in my head onto the paper. To make it more difficult, I couldn't spell the simplest words. I was in the sixth grade. I should know how to read and spell three and four syllable words, and I still didn't know most one-syllable words.

That year, Mother took us four younger children to the farm for a week at Easter. Most of the furniture was gone, but we still had a cook stove, and a bed in each bedroom. Although we were out of school, West Virginia wasn't. I was walking through the field by the schoolhouse when I thought I would look in. I opened the door and peeked into the building. At the front of the room a blackboard was hanging on the wall. An organ sat in the corner, and the wood stove was in the middle of the room. The kids sat on one side of the wood stove.

Hearing the squeaking door, the teacher looked up and was startled to see me. I turned away, but she called me to come in. The fire in the wood stove felt warm and I was cold, so I went in. She asked my name and where I had come from. The seven children looked at me while I answered her questions. Then I asked what she was teaching. She said, "The ABC's. Would you like to teach them to the children?"

For some reason, which to this day I can't explain, I said, "Yes, I would." The teacher handed me the letters, and I held some of them up while the children said them. But soon, I felt very uneasy. It made me feel uncomfortable to be watched by all those eyes. I said my good-byes and left quickly.

One morning while we were at the farm, I woke to the sound of singing. I could hear a very high voice, singing off key, and the organ hitting the wrong notes. The sounds filled the quietness outside. Soon I heard a man's voice yelling. I realized then that I was hearing the Easter Sunday service, which was held in the little schoolhouse. I had lost track of time, as I often did.

After Easter vacation my teacher told the class that we were going on a field trip to visit the Junior-Senior High School. While we were on the field trip, Miss Carter told us the whole class was going on to the seventh grade. I was both relieved and uneasy. Changes were very frightening and the idea of meeting new people in a new school scared me. Besides, I didn't want to leave my teacher.

In those days I was always afraid and learned early not to show my feelings. I felt lonely and lost much of the time, and had learned to withdraw rather than fight back. I could tell what people thought of me, what they wanted, and more important, what they didn't want. People either overestimated me or underestimated me and I learned to defend myself from either extreme.

I lived in terror that somebody somewhere was going to ask me to read or write something. This happened sometimes and when it did, I got something in my eye or started to clown around and make

14

people laugh. When they didn't feel like laughing, they would get annoyed with me because I was so silly.

Because I was immature and didn't appear to be very intelligent, I was capable of far more than school people thought I was. They did not pay any attention to my thoughts on any subject. If I asked questions, they were dismissed. I asked few questions, for I had lost interest in most things. If I did want to know something, I was afraid to ask.

Even my speech was affected by my learning problem. Not only did I not know the meaning of most long words, I was beginning to speak fast and slur my words. I wasn't able to pronounce what I could not hear. Pressure caused my mind to race, but the thoughts wouldn't come out right, either in speech or in writing.

The summer before I went into seventh grade, we were back at the farm. I went to church services in the little schoolhouse. At the beginning of the service, the minister asked for testimony. He wanted someone to get up and speak about how the Lord had saved them.

"From what?" I asked my cousin.

"Be quiet," she whispered.

After the service, the people of the church went around to each person and asked him or her if they were a Christian. Before they got to me, I asked my cousin what a Christian was. "Have you been baptized?" she asked. I didn't know what she was talking about, so I said I had.

When they got to me and asked if I was a Christian, I answered "Yes."

My cousin said she wasn't. They talked her into going to the front of the church. She knelt down and was crying. There were three or four people around her. It scared me to death and I didn't want any more of that.

Chapter 3
Junior High and High Schools

Junior High School brought new pressures. I made a few friends at the beginning, but that didn't last long. The kids I knew best in my classes were the boys I had traveled through school with. In the seventh grade, the kids really began to compete with each other and I was competing with no one. The way we dressed also became very important and since my father's drinking habit had become even worse, money was just not available to buy clothes. My sister Norma, who had a job, kept my brother and me in clothes as much as she could. My older brothers and sisters had jobs to help take care of the family.

I felt bad that I couldn't dress well and have friends. But that was nothing compared to my feelings about school itself. In elementary school where other kids learned the basic foundations, I had learned almost nothing. In the upper grades, where these basic skills are used to gather information and keep up with studies, I had nothing to build on. I was totally lost.

By eighth grade, the work became harder fast. I took English, Social Studies, Math, Science, Gym, Home Economics, Art and Music. It was a good thing for me that I had Gym, in which I was fairly good, and Home Economics, even though my sewing was awful, or I would have gone right out of my mind. In these classes, reading and spelling were not required often. In music we sang mostly. I did not have a singing voice, did not like to sing and could not learn the words to songs, not even popular songs that I had heard on the radio.

English was my most difficult class. The teacher did a lot of teaching with the use of the blackboard, mostly diagramming sentences. I sat in the last row of the classroom. Since I couldn't read or understand what was on the blackboard, the teacher had trouble holding my attention.

At times, she would read to us from Shakespeare, which I enjoyed very much, until it became hard for me to listen to. The written word was almost like another language to me. I didn't understand some of the sentences. Then I would feel lost and confused. When the frustration began to grow, I would stop listening.

Generally, I have a very good memory and it was the only thing I could count on. It is strange that my memory could not be counted on when it came to reading, spelling, dates or math facts. I could study words very closely, and study and study more, and still not be able to retain the spelling of them. My reading words totaled less than 150 and my spelling words even less than that. I could guess at some words, such as "then," "there," "those," "when," "where," "what," but I didn't really know them and couldn't spell some of them.

I had good days and bad days, which seemed to depend on the amount of information fed into my mind or the number of words I had to learn. Some days I could spell the words fairly well, but there were days when, for no reason I could understand, I couldn't get any of them right, even though the amount of study in both cases may have been the same. This happened in my class work, too. I would sometimes know the answer to a question the teacher would ask orally. Much of the time, though, I didn't know what the teacher was talking about.

I learned to take advantage of every situation. In ninth grade, I had study hall before English class. I would study the ten spelling words before I went to class on the day of the test. They were not hard words for a ninth grader, and I could get eight, nine or ten out of ten right on my test. But when it came time for the review test that had 50 to 100 words, I would get maybe seven correct. One time I got 17 out of 75 right.

The teacher was confused about this and told me to see her after class. She then told me I should study harder. Later in the year she told the class that even though I had missed one or two out of ten words, I did better than anyone in the class because I was a person who had great trouble with spelling. It was hard for her to understand that I simply couldn't cram that many words into my head.

None of the teachers understood that the more pressure I was under, the less I could do in the classroom. If I were extra tired, I would not retain any information. The tiredness came from the pressure at school, because I went to bed at 9 o'clock every night. None of my teachers seemed to understand that I didn't learn, but got information by cramming facts into my head. It confused them and added to the feeling that I was careless and lazy.

I don't think any of my teachers knew I couldn't read. They asked me how to spell "tranquility." I didn't know. After much study I learned how to spell it, but when I had to put it on the board, the teacher couldn't read my handwriting. He didn't ask me to repeat the letters I had written, but said sharply, "The word is wrong. Sit down." Of course my classmates found this really funny. To this day I have never forgotten how to spell "tranquility."

I did not learn the alphabet in order, and still get the letters mixed up when I write. I do this with words, too. When I write a sentence, I think I am writing one word when instead I write the word I am thinking about next. Or I may think I am writing, "am" and instead write "him." The longer I write, the more this happens. When I am tired or upset, it happens more often.

Only once in all my high school days did I get an "A" for my work. That was on the folder about my hometown. I worked very hard on it, cutting out articles from the newspaper and pasting them in the folder. The teacher in the class was very nice and he said I had done a beautiful job.

One of my classmates, who was an "A" student - the girl who had once made fun of me for not reading, overheard him and promptly said, "Don't you know why you got that "A"? It's for trying. The other kids don't try, but you do."

That "A" was like gold to me and she made it worthless. She made me feel that my work didn't deserve the "A", but that teacher had given it to me because he felt sorry for me.

Most of my high school marks were "D's," which was usually the grade given for trying. More and more I felt lonely and lost. One day one of the high school boys asked me to pose for nude pictures. He told me I could hide my head if I wanted to. It was then, at 16, that I told my mother I wanted to quit school. She just laughed. I knew then that she wasn't going to let me, so I went back without saying any more, but still hating every minute of it.

My family went to church even less in Cumberland than we had on the farm. We were not a religious family at that time, but when my older brother, who was in the Army, gave me a Gideon Bible, I began carrying it around with me at school. Before going into each class, I began to say the Lord's Prayer, which I had memorized, because we said it in school each morning. I prayed that I would not be called on to read or answer questions, and that no one would notice me. I wish I could say that the praying made things better, but it didn't. It did, however, make me want to know God. I didn't care about religion, but I wanted to learn about God himself.

One day when the Basic Math teacher asked me to read a problem and I couldn't read the words, I thought quickly and whispered, "I'm losing my voice." He went on to another student. At the end of class, he asked me why I carried the Bible with me. He was interested because he was a Sunday School teacher. I answered in my natural voice; "I read it." It wasn't a lie. Though it was a King James Version, I did try to read it. But the print was too small and the words too unfamiliar.

"Good!" he answered; not seeming to notice how quickly my hoarseness had disappeared.

Outside of my school my life was less pressured. I still preferred being outdoors when I could. Even the TV, which my father bought when I was in tenth grade, didn't interest me for long. Once the fascination with TV was over, I found TV programs to be as boring as radio.

My closet friends, like Anna, were in other classes and I saw them seldom during school. I did have friends outside the school and when money was available, I was able to do some things that I enjoyed, like going to football games.

In the eleventh grade, I was able to go to my Junior Prom only because I worked at the refreshment table. My sister, Betty, who is a very good seamstress, altered a dress, which one of my other sisters had worn as a bridesmaid. The gown was lavender and very pretty.

When Sue, a friend of mine, was sixteen, she got her driver's license and her father sometimes let her have the car. It was seldom that we got to go driving, but when we did, she would get fifty cents worth of gas and we would ride around from about 7 to 9 at night. She was very active in her church and talked about God and the church most of the time.

The happiest times of my childhood were spent with Anna's family. I loved Mr. and Mrs. Saylor and thought Mr. Saylor knew everything there was to know. During the warm weekends of fall and spring, we used to go to the Saylor's cabin in the West Virginia countryside. When there was a square dance, the Saylors would be sure I got to go. The square dances were every Saturday night and the whole family would go. Anna's grandfather was the caller and even her grandmother would go, as would most everyone in that small community of Paw Paw.

My mother had a stroke when I was seventeen. Every day after that, I could see her failing in her body and in her mind. It was very hard to watch and live with.

With school itself so painful, and mother's health getting worse, it meant a lot to me to get another good teacher in my last year of school. He taught psychology and tried to help me as much as he could. By that time, there was not much he could do, but he gave me some attention and kindness. He made me learn a poem, which was very hard for me because of my problem in hearing different sounds in words, and in memorizing rhyming words.

I worked extra hard to learn this poem because everyone in turn had to recite it in front of the class. When it was my turn, I was scared, as always, to be in front of the group, but I began to recite. Suddenly the boys started laughing, with the teacher joining in. I immediately froze. The teacher, seeing what was happening, told me they were laughing at something that happened in the hall outside the room. He kindly told me to sit down, that I could recite the poem to him later. This much of that poem is about the only thing I clearly remember learning in school:

Myself, by Edgar Guest

I have to live with myself and so,
I want to be fit for myself to know.
I want to be able as the days go by,
Always to look myself straight in the eye.
I don't want to keep on the closet shelf,
A lot of secrets about myself.
Fooling myself as I come and go,
Into thinking that nobody else will know.
The kind of man I really am,
I don't want to dress myself in sham.

He was a hard teacher. He demanded a lot and took no nonsense. One of the boys who sat behind me was pushing my chair out in the aisle. This went on for two classes. The room was always in order – no talking or misbehaving, so it was embarrassing to me. The boy would not stop no matter how many times I asked. The teacher ignored it for a while, then he walked by my chair, looked the boy in the eye, and said, "Don't you do that again." I knew the boy wouldn't do it again.

Although I lived in fear in those days, so much fear that I didn't know what I was afraid of, I never feared that my peers would lay hands on me or say unkind things to me. You could always hear a pin drop in that room. When that teacher spoke, his voice was all you heard. The fear of being called on to read or answer questions was always there, but I still liked him, as all of his students did.

It was in this psychology class that I learned, if I offered to read or answer a question, he would call on me and then leave me alone for the rest of the class. I had study hall before his class, so I would learn the answer to a question from a classmate or I would cram a paragraph, getting the words from a classmate. When I got to class I would volunteer to read the paragraph or answer the question. But sometimes this didn't work. He would ask me to read something when I hadn't volunteered, and I didn't know the words. After a short time he would tell me to stop. He seemed to be so confused.

School was almost over forever, but I had one more frightening experience to endure. At the middle of twelfth grade, my class was sent to the cafeteria to take a test given by a man I had never seen before. Later, I was called out of class to talk to the man who had given me the test. I was scared to death. Any test is very upsetting to me and to talk about it with the teacher meant I would be scolded. If anyone called me by my given name, "Dolores," I was being scolded, and though he began, "Dolores...," he did not scold me. He told me that I should read more often, taking words from the newspaper to build my vocabulary, and that I should seek employment as a clerk in a store, or some similar work, after graduation.

I had learned to hate school, education, and everyone that had anything to do with it, except for a few friends and special teachers. I graduated from high school ranking as the 267th student in a class of 272. I was the fifth lowest in my class, with an IQ of 69. Graduation meant one thing to me: I was finished with school forever.

Chapter 4
Evading Discovery

The day after graduation from high school, I went to Washington, D.C. where two of my sisters and two brothers were living. I had been set free from school and I loved it. Later that summer my sister-in-law and I began looking for work. At an employment agency I conned Helen into filling out my job application. Helen had no idea I could not read and write, so I had to be careful how I talked her into filling it out. Since we were always laughing and fooling around, it wasn't too hard. I asked her what she wrote for the first question. She answered, "My name."

I told her I was scared, quickly pushed the paper to her, and said, "Fill this thing out, I'm so nervous I don't know what I'm doing." She filled out the form for me, joking all the time.

We were sent to a bank for interviews and a test. When we returned to the employment agency, the woman who worked there still had her hat on, I noticed. I wondered why she wore it all the time. She remained seated, looked me up and down, then called a dry cleaning plant and told them, "I have a nice girl here who is clean, well-groomed and can work with her hands." I knew then that she must have gotten the results of the test at the bank. Finally she sent both Helen and me to an insurance company, where no test was given.

I got a job filing accident claims by number. Helen got a job in another office of the same company, which required more written work and more attention to details.

I began to realize how important reading was while I worked at this job. One day at the office, I was alone when a girl from another department asked me to check out a file. I had always found someone else to do this for me. Now I was trapped. I needed to know how to spell her name so I could sign the file out. I knew her name was in the checkout box and I looked quickly to find it. I could not find it, so I wrote it the best I could. Later one of the girls who worked with me saw it and demanded, "What does this say?"

"Jean," I answered.

"It does not," she said. I couldn't see what was wrong with it. She quickly erased my writing and rewrote it. It was easy to understand why she was so short with me.

My filing was not too good, either. I often misfiled files, and it would take a lot of time to find them. The girls were not sure that I was doing the misfiling since there were about ten of us. But I think they had a feeling I was the one.

One day I said "segregation" instead of "subrogation" (another department in the insurance company) and the girls laughed at me. One girl saw that I was hurt and said not to laugh at me. Another girl then said they weren't laughing at me, but with me.

The fear of someone finding out that I couldn't read was growing. At income tax time I talked my sister, Norma, into doing my taxes for me. Fortunately, it was a short form, and easy for her to do.

I always found ways to get my sisters to do those kinds of jobs for me. I stayed away from all reading and writing unless I couldn't get out of it. Being the youngest girl in my family made it easier. Besides, Norma, who was a secretary, was always telling me I killed the King's English.

When my sisters went to St. Luke's Methodist Church, I went with them. I never forgot about the Bible, and the Lord's Prayer I had learned in school. For some reason I hung onto it and I don't know why, but I still wanted to know about God. Although I went to church with my sisters, I wouldn't think of going to Sunday School. Even in church, I was afraid someone would call attention to me like they used to in the service in the little schoolhouse in West Virginia, when they called on people to give their testimony or to be saved. I was always very uneasy.

On December 2, 1955, we all went to a nightclub to celebrate a wedding anniversary in the family. We always went out in a large group and had a good time. On this evening, a guy who was in the Air Force asked me to dance. Later he and his friend joined our party. Jim asked if he could come to see me. He was pleasant and had a good sense of humor. We laughed a lot that evening. As a matter of fact, I saw him every night until March 3rd, when we were married. He was working with computers and seemed to be very intelligent, and I wondered what he saw in me. Before we were married I asked him. He said, "You are as cute as a speckled pup." He had no idea I couldn't read, and I wasn't about to tell him.

Jim and I spent our honeymoon in West Palm Beach, Florida, where he had been transferred. One day, not long after we were married, Jim said he would do the grocery shopping on the way home from the base if I would give him a list. He had taken me by surprise, so I just wrote some words, the best I knew how, on a piece of paper.

When Jim came home that night, having gotten the groceries, he said, "Did you see the way you wrote that list?" He thought I had done it as a joke. I don't remember what I said, or if I said anything. But I knew that now I would need to use other ways to get out of writing. Sometimes I would get mad or start a fight, although we didn't fight much, but most of the time I would just fool around and laugh.

When I did the shopping, which was not often, I had trouble reading cans, boxes and packages. I would buy tomato paste when I meant to buy tomato puree. I didn't know the difference until I opened the can. Then if it were paste, I would throw the full can away and cook something else, which did not call for tomato puree. I didn't know I could add water to the paste to thin it down.

Jim took care of all our money matters. He paid the bills and helped with the shopping. Cooking was one of his hobbies, and he took a lot of pains to fix everything just right, even to the seeding and slicing of grapes for a salad.

I could do only the easy cooking that I had been taught at home, since I couldn't read recipes. Jim liked to eat and he liked good food, so I was going to have to learn somehow. I began to watch others very closely as they cooked then try to do the same. However, I did make a lot of mistakes. I burned the packaged breakfast rolls one morning. After that, for a time, Jim called me "Cinde*roll*a."

After six months at West Palm Beach, Jim was discharged from the service and we returned to Washington. Jim got a job at the CIA and I went back to work at the same company where I had worked before, only in a different department.

We moved into an apartment in Glover Park and attended St. Luke's Methodist Church. Jim had gone to church all his life. Jimmy, our first son, was born in January of 1958. The next year, I was pregnant again and Mark was born in March of 1959. I was twenty-three when our third son, Paul, was born in June, 1960. I knew nothing about babies or how to care for them, and here I was with three! The books and the directions the doctor gave me did no good, since I couldn't read them.

It was then, with the boys to care for, that my fear and guilt and frustration really grew. After Jimmy was born, I unknowingly put too much dextromaltrose in his formula. He had terrible diarrhea and I was very worried. Luckily, my sister-in-law was visiting one day and watched me make his formula. She was surprised and asked me why I was putting so much dextromaltrose in his formula. She told me the difference between a heaping teaspoon and a level teaspoon. I never made that mistake again.

Of course, I had trouble reading the labels on medicines. I would mistake tablespoons and teaspoons. So I listened closely to the doctor when he gave me medicines or prescriptions so that I would know how much medicine to give. Jim thought I was a good mother with a lot of sense. I couldn't stand for him to know I couldn't read, but it took all my will power and know-how to keep it from him.

I refused to do any writing and Jim wrote to his mother every week. I was "too busy" to be writing - a new mother and all. If my sisters called for a recipe from a cookbook Norma had bought me, I would hand the cookbook to Jim. He enjoyed talking to them about the recipes and never minded reading it to them.

The people living at our apartment building were older, and/or employed, so I had no one my age with whom I could talk. I was very lonely, and was even becoming afraid to leave the apartment alone, except to visit my sisters, who lived one block from us. I didn't like being out alone and being responsible for the boys.

Jim never liked to care for an infant, even his own, and wouldn't help with the boys when they were babies. At that time, I was also caring for my mother at my apartment during the day because my sisters were working. Mother had another stroke and this added to my worries. My biggest fears at that time were that my mother might die, that something might happen to my children, and that someone might find out I could not read.

Now Jimmy began walking and I had to be careful of household containers that were poisonous, so I never knowingly bought anything that had poison in it.

Because Norma worked for the Department of Agriculture, she told me about certain chemicals and ingredients that had been thought harmless and had turned out to be dangerous; if I felt a certain thing might be harmful, I took no chances, I didn't buy it. I was afraid all chemicals were harmful. Fear became a way of life for me.

Jim was growing unhappy with his job as a computer operator at the CIA and wanted to better himself with another job. So in the summer of 1960 when Paul was only four weeks old, we moved to Los Angeles. There, Jim was able to get a job with the Veterans Administration right away.

It was in Los Angeles that the presidential nominating convention was held that year. I took a great fancy to John F. Kennedy because he seemed to have a way of speaking that made things clear. In my thinking, he could speak almost as well as Martin Luther King. My father had been a strong Republican. His friends called him "Democrat Smith" to tease him. I began carrying on the family tradition of being interested in politics, getting all of my information from TV. My interest in the world's problems was growing by leaps and bounds. I had always thought that segregation was wrong, and got mad every time I thought about it.

Our apartment in Los Angeles was a small one-bedroom apartment with a living room/kitchen combination. I thought I would make it more livable for the five of us if I could decorate it. I bought an interior-decorating book and tried to teach myself to read it. It was hopeless, so I gave up and looked at the pictures.

After living in Los Angeles for fifteen months, we decided to return to Washington. We hadn't learned to like Los Angeles. The lifestyle was lonely and unfamiliar. At the time of our return, I was seven months pregnant.

This time, we moved into a seven-room house outside of Georgetown. The house was owned by St. Luke's Church. The minister, responding to a letter that Jim had written telling of our return to Washington, said we could rent the house for $100 a month.

Soon after returning, word came that my mother was in a coma and dying. My doctor would not give me permission to travel at that time, so I stayed behind while my brothers and sisters went to be with her. Mother died November 15, 1961 and John was born December 8, 1961.

That same year the three older boys came down with the old-fashioned measles. There was so much talk on TV and radio about the danger of measles and possible brain damage as a result, that I was frightened. I will never understand why simple language is not used on TV and radio when it is important to reach and educate all people. So often after the first five or six sentences, I wouldn't know what the people on TV and radio were talking about. They were vague and used too many words I didn't understand.

My fear and guilt about not knowing how to read and write never stopped growing. Everything that happened, such as my boys' illnesses, added to it. Each day I was hiding from those closest to me, even my husband. I couldn't write business or personal letters or checks. I could "read" my mother-in-law's letters, simply because I knew her so well I could guess what she was going to say. Sometimes, though, I would tell Jim things in the letter that never happened.

I couldn't read about drugs, smoking, and changes in laws, mercury poison, or the danger of bug spray. I couldn't read or answer notices or notes or fill out forms the boys brought home from school, no matter how important they were. And I could not get a driver's license. In other words, if reading had to be done, I couldn't do it. Because of people's poor opinions of those who can't read or write, I felt better hiding it.

Chapter 5
To Tell the Truth

I could tell Jim felt there was something wrong, although we never talked about it. I was always afraid I had failed as a mother, and I was very unhappy. I didn't like myself; I didn't trust anyone, and I didn't know where to turn. In the past, I had been good humored and laughed a lot. When I was a kid, Mrs. Saylor was always telling me and everyone else that I was always the same.

But that had changed, because of the responsibility that I felt for the boys, and the fact that I was always there with them. Jim should know, but I couldn't find the courage to tell him.

We now fought a lot. I screamed at the kids, and hit them far too much. When Jim and I got into a fight, he would win, using three-syllable words I did not know. Since I didn't know what he was talking about, I thought I was wrong and he was right.

I had heard people talk about God all my life. Mother had talked about God a lot, but to me it was only talk. I didn't understand any of it. I had gone to church occasionally with the Saylors and another friend, because nearly everyone went and it seemed the thing to do. Sometimes I would hear a story of hope, one of the miracles, and was told that if I prayed, Jesus, who was the Son of God, would help me if I believed in Him and asked for help. Most of the time though, I didn't understand the stories I heard from the Bible.

When Jim again became active at St. Luke's Methodist Church, I rarely went, because I still had a fear of having attention called to myself. I learned people can be unkind to a young mother who has had four children in four years. The look on their faces told me what they thought. I found it much easier to send the boys with Jim and stay home.

But when I did go to church, I enjoyed hearing our new minister, Dr. W. Hedley Clews, even though his large vocabulary was hard for me to understand. Fortunately, he made it a point to know his people and he soon visited us. He was a warm, loving person with deep blue eyes, a broad smile and a delightful sense of humor. He would get up at five every morning and study until nine o'clock. He was a lover of history, the Bible, and philosophy. From the start, I enjoyed being with him and talking to him. I felt the love he had in him and knew I could trust him.

Jim was working a part time job in addition to his regular job, and I didn't see him much. With all the energy I had, I could clean the house in no time, which left me with lots of time to think. I would walk from room to room, thinking about God.

One night as I stood at the sink washing dishes and thinking about the warnings of poisons that children could take in a home, a wave of hopelessness came over me and I felt that I couldn't go on any more. How was I to know what was poisonous and what was not? I wasn't fit to raise children and I couldn't stand the fear any longer. I leaned on the counter and cried, "Help me God. I don't care what you do with me, just help me." It was not out of love that I turned to God. It was out of desperation and with the hope that if Jesus was who He said He was, He would help me. The light in the room became brighter and in that moment I knew He heard me.

I needed to know about this God more than ever, so I listened very carefully to Dr. Clews' sermons. In one of them he said, "If you want something badly enough to work sixteen hours a day for it, it's yours". I wanted to read the Bible to learn about this God who was going to set me free, so that I could make up my own mind what I thought of Him and what He wanted from me. The desire to learn to read consumed me. Each day I tried to read the Bible, opening it at random, but it took the whole week to figure out enough of the one verse I was reading to make any sense from it. John 15:7 is where it opened to the most, "If you abide in me, and my words abide in you, ask whatever you will and it shall be done for you." It is a good thing that God doesn't want anything from us but ourselves, because I wouldn't have known what to give Him.

I began to go to church regularly. I loved to see Dr. and Mrs. Clews and talk to them. They would not accept anything from me but my best. Dr. Clews was always challenging my thinking. He introduced me to people like Plato, Socrates, Eric Hoffer, and gave me more understanding of Shakespeare. Though I thought a lot, I had trouble putting my thoughts into words. I tried to do it out loud and in this way I began to sort out and take in new thoughts and make sense of them. To this day I use new words and thoughts by speaking them aloud to take hold of them, but I find I need to do it less and less. Once I understand a complete thought, I don't forget it.

I was learning more and more now. The more I learned, the more I wanted to learn. I was watching TV and listening to the radio most of the time. I would hear something that I wanted to learn about and in the middle of it one of the boys would say something or get into a fight; when I couldn't hear what was being said on radio or TV, I would scream at the boys to leave me alone because I knew I would not hear it again. It would be gone forever.

Where my patience stopped, Jim's took over. He was able to talk quietly with the boys when I was angry and frustrated, and play with them when I just wanted to be left alone. Jim also took the boys shopping for all of their clothes, and at other times would bring home little treats for them. His strong support for the boys helped me, too.

Even with Jim's help with the boys, I quite frankly hated being alive. I hated to go to bed at night because I would have to get up in the morning and live through another day. Mrs. Clews helped me through those days.

One night when I was at my lowest, I went to bed and picked up a copy of "The Upper Room" that was lying on Jim's nightstand. I opened it up and for some reason unknown to me at the time. I was able to read the bold print which said, "The Spirit Must Grow." I was simply amazed that I could read the phrase.

My sister, Norma, was painting, so I decided to give it a try. I painted every day, but it was hard and I was not good at it. I couldn't break down the pictures I was copying, pull out the details, and paint them on the canvas. As hard as it was, I kept after it.

Meanwhile, I told Mrs. Clews, who also painted, about my painting. She looked at my pictures and encouraged me to keep on painting. I got into the habit of calling her on the phone almost every day, and we would sometimes talk as long as an hour at a time. One night I decided to tell Mrs. Clews I couldn't read. Even though I loved her, it took all my courage to tell her; but I knew she would understand, for she had a great ability to love people. I told her that as a child I couldn't learn in school and had never learned to read. Since she had been an elementary school teacher, she offered to help me. "Don't ever stop trying," she told me.

"If I had enough courage to tell you, I will never stop trying," I answered.

Later that night, Dr. Clews gave me a book on grammar and told me if ever he could help, to feel free to call him. Mrs. Clews worked with me two or three times, but when she found out how poor I was in reading and spelling, she was afraid she would do more harm than good.

Our oldest son Jimmy was in the first grade and Mark in Kindergarten. City life in general was very frightening to me because the city is too big and confusing and lonely. There was no one I could go places with. I had a very nice neighbor with two children, but her husband worked on Capitol Hill and I felt uneasy with her. I still had fear of going out alone and became more afraid every day. Finally I talked Jim into moving. He didn't want to, but agreed because I wanted to so badly. In October 1964, we bought a home in Gaithersburg, Maryland. I was 28 years old.

After I had told Mrs. Clews I couldn't read, I finally had the courage to tell Jim and ask him to help me. I don't think he was too surprised. He said he would try to help me learn to read, but he felt he wasn't good at that kind of thing. He was right. He went to the Gaithersburg Library and got a junior high school grammar book. As soon as I saw the size of it, I knew that thick book wasn't for me! Jim didn't say anything to me, or anyone else, about my being illiterate, though I could tell that it bothered him.

For a time I thought my problem was spelling. If I could just learn to spell, surely I could then learn to read. Somehow there must be a way, even though no one had yet been able to help me. I bought some workbooks on a first grade level at the drug store and tried to teach myself. I just couldn't do it.

Meanwhile Mrs. Clews had contacted a friend who lived in Gaithersburg within walking distance of us. She was a teacher who was working with children with learning handicaps and was willing to help me.

When I went to see her, we had lunch by candlelight, which was delightful. She talked to me for a long time about reading, after which she asked me to read. She said I was intelligent and could learn to read, but I hadn't been taught the sounds of letters. She gave me phonics workbooks on a third grade level, which I was to take home and work on. That was the first time I had ever heard of phonics. I picked up a few words, but it wasn't getting any easier. I still couldn't read many of the simplest words, such as "map," "leg," "cut," etc.

Also I still didn't really know the difference between words which looked much alike, like "then/there," "this/that," "when/what," "which/where." Although I was guessing better than ever before and was fooling my teacher, I was growing more and more afraid that I just could not learn to read. I wouldn't say much to her about how hard it was, because I was afraid she would tell me I couldn't learn.

She seemed to lose her enthusiasm for helping me when I wasn't able to learn the way she thought I should, so I quit going to see her.

My life had improved in other areas, though, for the same day we had moved into our house, I felt like a bird out of a cage. Mary Shay had moved into a house down the street that same day. I had someone to go places with. I didn't need to go out alone. It didn't take long for Mary and me to become the best of friends.

Even so, it was two years before I asked her to help me. We were shopping and I asked her if she would like for me to tell her a secret. "I can't read," I said.

She looked at me and said nothing for a minute. Then she said, "You're kidding."

"No," I answered, "I'm not."

She picked up a book from a shelf, opened it and asked, "What is this word?"

"I don't know," I answered.

She then pointed to another word and asked again, "What is this word?"

I told her I didn't know. I said, "Mary, I am not kidding. I can't read."

She closed the book, put it back on the shelf, and said nothing more about it for several days. I wondered if she had lost respect for me, but she acted like it didn't bother her. Then I told her about the teacher who had been trying to teach me to read. I told Mary I knew the teacher didn't understand my problem. Mary was very kind. I asked her if she would help me. She said she would.

Until Mary actually tried to help me, she couldn't believe that I was not able to read. She got workbooks on a first grade level from a nun she knew. Mary worked with me more than anyone else. She felt I didn't sit still long enough to learn to read. I thought she was partially right. But kind as she was, we got nowhere fast.

My sister Betty gave me a workbook on grammar because she was tired of the way I talked. She didn't know I couldn't read and was trying to learn. She said I talked the way I did because I didn't look at words carefully when I read. For instance, I would say "bluecoats" for "glucose."

With each of my teachers I worked very hard at first, even at grammar. They were all convinced now that if I wanted to learn, I would. All of them felt that my only problem was a lack of confidence in myself. They didn't know how long I had wanted to learn to read, or how hard I had tried. And believe me, I had tried; I tried for years. They all thought I could learn the way they had learned. No one had any idea how deep the problem went, how much patience it took, and how long it took to work on the smallest words and sounds to be able to build a foundation and move on.

I was asked by the Youth Director of our church to teach a Junior/Senior High Sunday School class. I don't know why I said yes, but I wanted to try it. It was the first time I had been in a Sunday School class since that awful day before sixth grade when I was asked to read.

I had been teaching for about six months when I told the Youth Director I couldn't read and was trying to learn. I'll never forget the look on his face. Then he said, "Mrs. Howell, don't try to learn to read any longer. Stay the way you are. You are just fine."

I was so shocked to hear him say those words. Why would I want to stay the way I was, unable to read? "No," I said, "I have to learn to read."

I continued to try to read the Bible. The Youth Director gave me a *GOOD NEWS FOR MODERN MAN* Bible, because he thought the simple language might be helpful. I loved it, but it was still too hard to read. Maybe someday, I thought, as I looked through it. I used it so much, trying to read it, that in six months it was falling apart. He gave me another one. He told me jokingly that it was expensive to buy me a Bible every six months.

Although I could not read the Bible, or anything else, to prepare my Sunday School lessons, I picked up a lot from listening closely. I paid close attention to what others said, and bluffed the rest of the way through. For three years I taught Junior and Senior High Sunday School.

I will never understand the faith that Dr. and Mrs. Clews had in me. They knew I couldn't read, and they never let me know how concerned they were. Whenever I asked for help, they gave it, but never until they were asked.

As I struggled with my Sunday School class, my boys were beginning their own struggles. In the fall of 1967, Jimmy was in the fourth grade, Mark in the third, Paul in second and John in first. Jimmy seemed to be unhappy. Although I was still not a patient mother, I was a concerned one. I wanted my boys to be happy. I tried to find out why Jimmy was not happy, but I couldn't put my finger on the problem. He was not happy either at home or school. In the winter of that year, Paul got an ulcer. Though it cleared up with medication, I had become uneasy about him, and all of them, in their schooling. Something was wrong, but I didn't know what.

The previous year, John's kindergarten teacher had called me to school for a conference. She said he was very immature. I suggested taking him out and waiting until the next year, but the teacher convinced me not to. She said that in an ungraded school like that one, he would go on with children like himself and catch up later.

But when I was called in during his first grade about his immaturity, I was sorry I had listened to the kindergarten teacher. I felt he would have been better off if he had waited a year to start first grade. His first grade teacher and I agreed to work on his immaturity by giving him more responsibilities. I thought time helped immaturity, not responsibilities, but at that point, I thought the schools knew more than I did, so I said nothing.

It was time to move again. Gaithersburg had changed. It was no longer a small town. Maybe a new school would be better. Once more I asked Jim if we could move to a less crowded area, and once more he agreed.

This time we moved to the country, and bought a home in Boyds, Maryland. Taylor School in our new community was very small, with a class size of about sixteen. I felt better. It was a relief to have my boys in a different school.

Soon after we moved, late in March, I heard of a class in the public school system for illiterates and called one of the ministers in the area for information. When he learned it was for me, he said, "...but I can tell by talking to you that you don't need that class." Then I called my sister Norma who worked for "HELP," to find out more about the classes. She was in a hurry, said that I didn't know anyone who was illiterate, and hung up. Then the whole thing began to seem funny and I didn't care who knew that I couldn't read.

It was now 1968, and I asked everyone, anywhere I could think of, for help and still no one understood the problem.

Finally, I learned of a class ten miles away. I was told it was a reading class, but in fact it was a class preparing for the High School Equivalency test. Since I couldn't drive, I asked my sister, Betty, to drive me there once a week.

The teacher put me to work on about sixth grade material, and so it was a time for me to try and fool my teacher, because I knew she didn't understand me. The materials were rather easy to guess about, once I got used to them, mostly because they were stories on how we should live our lives. I was not about to let the other students know how bad my reading was, if I could help it. Luckily, good common sense covered up much of my inability to read.

The teacher tried to help, and I was sure she was going to say, "Dolores, you are guessing." But like all the others in the past she didn't understand my problem and had no idea I was guessing.

I stayed with it for over one year. I didn't read out loud often and when I did, the time was very short so I didn't have to read very much. The teacher thought I was doing well. I remember writing a paper only one time, getting help from Jim on how to spell words. Even with help I misspelled a lot and my penmanship was poor.

I told the teacher I couldn't spell, that I couldn't even spell "spell." It went right over her head. The class was losing students and when it got down to three of us, I didn't want to go back. One night we were talking about Roosevelt being elected as President and I said that he had been elected to four terms. The teacher thought for a minute and said that was right.

One of the girls, a black girl with big brown eyes and a good sense of humor, turned to me and said, "You are the smartest thing I ever seen." I just looked at her. It took me by surprise because she was very sharp and a good student. She passed her GED test after that, and I never saw her again.

In the fall, after our move from Gaithersburg, Jim went alone to the first PTA meeting at Taylor School. There he learned from the boys' teachers that all four were far behind in reading, but might catch up that year if they worked hard. When Jim told me, a dreadful fear came over me. I spent the next week afraid and confused, too frightened to talk about it with Jim or anyone else.

Not long after that, the principal called to ask me to teach art after school. I was shocked to have a principal ask me to teach anything in school. He had heard through Mark that I had won some prizes with my paintings. I told him I would be glad to teach, but he should know that I couldn't read. He said that didn't matter, because I would not need to do any reading. That too, surprised me. I thought that in school all you did was read and write.

Soon the principal called again, this time to ask for permission for psychological testing for Jimmy. When he asked if the school psychologist could visit me, I was terrified, for I had never before talked to a psychologist. Psychology to me meant something wrong with the brain. I prayed and prayed, "Please, please help me God."

After a while the fear lifted enough that I could talk to her. She asked a lot of questions and took many notes. We talked about my paintings, my church work, and the boys' births and medical history. The births had been normal, the boys' weights were good, and I had never smoked nor drank. At the end she said, "This is the most encouraging home I've been in for quite a while." She made me feel that there was hope, and that my fear would go away.

Jim trusted the school system completely. There was no question in his mind that his boys would be taught, as he had been taught, to read, write, spell and learn math very well.

Soon after the psychologist's visit, Jim and I were called to school for a conference. The psychologist told us that if Jimmy's reading problem could be corrected, he could be above average in all areas. A few weeks later, she called to suggest a reading tutor for Jimmy. I had no idea then how this suggestion would change my life.

Until this conference, we didn't know that Jimmy had as serious a disability as she was talking about. The staff at Rosemont, where he had been going, never told us anything like this, and when the teacher at Taylor was so concerned, I asked Mary Shay to read Jimmy's past report cards to see if we could tell from them whether he had this kind of problem. Mary said the report cards didn't indicate the problem.

I didn't know what to think, or what lay ahead. I had had a lot of frustration in my life, but I didn't know there was as much frustration and loneliness in this whole world as I was going to feel for the next many years. I still couldn't take the driver's test, even after three learner's permits. I couldn't read the rulebook, but now for the first time the book had the questions and answers in the back. I knew I had to get that driver's license because the tutor for Jimmy lived in Gaithersburg, ten miles away. With Jim and Mary helping me, I spent the next weeks pouring over the book, matching the questions with the answers. I also had a problem with parking, so Jim found an instructor to teach me. The instructor said he would take me in his car when I was ready for the test.

On the Thursday I was to take the test, the instructor couldn't come. What a relief it was to put off the test until Monday, because I didn't have the strength yet to go through with it. I had been so scared and upset I did not know how I was going to get through that test. Now I would have the weekend to get ready.

I prayed and prayed. As I thought about the test, the words came to me: "When you give one slice of bread to God, the whole loaf is His." On Monday I passed the test, with a score of 100. The officer who gave me my driving test was so kind and gentle, and kindness with someone like me can make the difference between passing and failing any test, no matter how well prepared I was.

God had led me to this point. Another part of my life began with the beginning of Jimmy's tutoring. Mrs. Jean Temple, his tutor, made the first appointment for after Christmas. Jimmy would work with her three times a week.

At the first lesson, Mrs. Temple told me that many children have similar problems and that it is more common among boys. She had seen this in her work on the staff of the Kingsbury Center in Washington. She talked about consonant and vowel sounds, but I didn't fully understand what she was talking about. One thing, though, was clear to me: SHE knew what she was talking about, and I needed her help too.

After Jimmy's second lesson, I turned to Mrs. Temple and said, "Maybe someday you can help me, because I want to read the Bible more than anything else in the world." I told her I thought I read at about first grade level, and right away she said she would try to help.

I couldn't believe it, for I had met with such frustration for so long. Because I had never been able to get anyone to believe how bad my problem was, I had finally stopped trying. I knew it was more than a grammar problem or lack of self-confidence, but no one else seemed to believe that. It had seemed to me so hopeless, and now here at last was someone who did understand.

At first I didn't know where the money was going to come from, for we had just bought a house and Jim had to buy me a car. Mrs. Temple helped with that, too. She asked only what we could afford for Jimmy.

Mrs. Temple did some informal testing with me. She asked me to read and write three letter words, which I could not do. She recognized my inability to hear vowel and consonant sounds as well as my difficulty in reading and writing. Gently she told me I was right about the first grade level. After a moment, she added that an adult as handicapped as I was might not ever be able to learn to read. She asked me if I had ever heard the word "dyslexia."

I told her I hadn't. Then I found the courage to ask her how close I was to being retarded. In her gentle way, she said that being unable to read did not mean I was retarded. I was 32 years old, and it was the biggest relief of my life to hear those words. Then an awful thought came: had I come all this way only to be told I couldn't learn to read? "Oh God, I hope not," I thought. I held tight to Him and did what I had to do.

Jim also talked to Mrs. Temple. Until that time he really didn't know how bad my problem was. It was funny. No one knew I couldn't read until I told them, and then no one would believe it because I had them so well fooled.

Chapter 6
A Break Though at Last

I had spent 26 years trying to learn why I was unable to learn. Now I knew. In that week following my first visit with Jean Temple, waves of the past, all the ups and downs of my life washed over me. The question that kept surfacing was, "Will my children have to go through this, too?"

Jimmy and I were both being tutored three times a week, for an hour each time. During a six-month period, Jimmy finally, in the fifth grade, learned consonant blends (such as bl and tr) and short vowel sounds for the first time. By June, he was beginning to use them in both reading and spelling. He also went from a first grade to a second grade reading level.

For me, the work was by far the most tiring I had ever done in my life. Jean discovered that I was not only handicapped in reading and spelling, but in other areas as well. This meant that I had a learning disability in addition to dyslexia, which is the inability to read, write, spell and sometimes speak normally. I learned that I have a poor concept of numbers. I could only tell time on the five-minute marks and even then I had trouble, and still do, with the numbers between the six and the twelve.

I also had difficulty distinguishing between the words I heard which sounded alike, such as cone/comb, death/deaf, awnings/onyx, jury/jewelry, and counter/calendar. In addition, I often mispronounced the prefixes and suffixes.

I spoke the way I THOUGHT I heard the words, as when I told my neighbor, I liked the onyx over her window. I have always known the word "sympathy," but never could pronounce the word "symphony."

Mary was calling for tickets to a symphony for the four of us and I told her that I could not pronounce that word. She wrote it on a piece of paper, showed me the "ph" and with practice I learned to say it, but when it came time for me to buy a sympathy card for Jim's uncle, I had lost *that* word. To this day I cannot pronounce "sympathy" because I get the two words mixed up.

As I worked with Mrs. Temple, and learned more about dyslexia, my own problems came into focus. I have always liked to use quotations, but have learned that I often get them incorrect or backwards, such as "take a short walk off a long pier," or "a bush in the hand is worth two birds," or "don't buy a poke in a pig."

I don't always know my left hand from my right. I tried to remember that my wedding ring is on my left hand. Once when Jean Temple asked me to show her how long three feet would be, I answered that my arms weren't long enough.

Although I painted, I couldn't draw and had to trace my pictures. My memory for names, faces and directions is very poor. I also had great trouble with abstract reasoning. The Bible was very hard for me to understand. In the twenty-third Psalm:

"The Lord is my Shepherd
I shall not want,
He maketh me to lie down in green pastures."

I didn't know what these lines meant. I couldn't make the connection.

Mrs. Temple knew her business. She went right to the heart of the problem, and her understanding of how hard it was for me, as well as her delightful sense of humor were the things which kept me going. I know it was almost as hard for her to reach me as for me to take hold of those sounds and words. After tutoring me for two months, she asked me, "What is a vowel?"

My answer was "The name of a person, place or thing."

She laid her head on the table and cried, "I failed, I failed."

Sometime later, I couldn't learn the word "drugged." She would write these words that I could not learn on little pieces of paper and show them to me at each lesson. But no matter how many times she would show me "drugged," I couldn't get it. Finally, in complete frustration, she took the piece of paper, slowly tore it into pieces and sang out, "I don't care if you never learn this word." In that moment, I learned it.

When she gave me three and four letter words, I just couldn't do them well. She started with the short "a" as in "apple' sound. She would use all my senses: seeing, hearing and feeling for words. It was much more tiring than hard physical work and I felt exhausted all the time. I even dreamed about words and sounds, but they were never in any form or pattern.

One day Jean gave me a list of five letter words. On the list were the words "bread" and "beard." She asked me what the difference was in these two words.

"There is no difference," I answered.

She asked again, "What is the difference in these two words?"

And again I answered, "There is no difference. They are the same words."

The third time she asked, this time using a pencil and pointing to each letter, "What is the difference?" For a moment I couldn't believe what I was seeing. Why hadn't I been able to see that? My eyes were better than 20/20. But I couldn't see the difference until she showed me the "r" and I could see the letters were in a different place. I never knew that I was mixing up letters until Jean would tell me that I would say "was" for "saw," "on" for "no" and so on.

I would often stare at words that she was trying to teach me, wondering why I couldn't learn what seemed so easy for everyone else. She would have a hard time pulling my attention back to her. There are so many words, I thought, and I could hardly learn these few. After a moment, Jean would ask what bothered me about a certain word that I was staring at. "I don't know," I would say, and we went on.

When my mind would get so tired and I didn't think I could stand it any longer, Jean would take my hand and say, "I know this is hard." That was all she had to say; I knew she understood. When she saw that my eyes were glassy, she told me, and stopped the tutoring. I told her I didn't know how she could have so much patience. "There's no way I'll ever be a tutor," I told her. She agreed.

I cannot begin to describe how hard it was for me to learn. If I was upset or felt bad or drank too much coffee, which caused my mind to race faster than I could deal with, I would lose all I had learned and we would have to start that lesson all over again.

At first, reading was so hard I wasn't getting anything out of it. Although my reading comprehension was very high, I didn't enjoy what I was reading until Mrs. Temple got books on a third grade level about people, such as Hans Christian Anderson, Laura Bridgeman, Thomas Jefferson, and others. I liked to read about people and how they overcame their problems. Jean would read one paragraph and I would read the other, until we got through the book.

After being tutored for quite some time, I picked up one of Jim's books, *COMMON SENSE*, by Thomas Payne. It was a small book, and I opened it up and tried to read it. When Jim came home, I asked him to read the first two pages to me. I was so fascinated with one part that for the next two days I tried to read it over and over, but found it impossible. The words were:

"Society in every state is a blessing, but Government, even in its best state, is but a necessary evil; in its worst state, an intolerable one; and when we suffer, or are exposed to the same miseries by a government, which we might expect in a country without government, our calamity is heightened by reflecting that we furnish the means by which we suffer."

I took the book to tutoring with me and Jean was so taken aback she asked me where I got it. I said I found it at home. She told me I had accomplished a lot so far, but what is to come is going to be far more interesting.

Even though I could by now read the Bible better, I would not read for enjoyment. I had to make myself read and I couldn't keep at it for long, even if I knew most of the words.

However, my memory was getting stronger. I would watch the TV news, or listen to the radio all day long. I knew that I couldn't remember all the things that I heard, so I would not hold on to things that I didn't think were important.

As my memory got stronger, I was getting impatient with others who didn't have good memories. I often told Jim and Mark their memories were about one inch long.

I also questioned everything, including the Bible. Dr. Clews and I would spend hours discussing the Bible. He told me I was full of questions up to my ears. He seemed to enjoy talking with me. He told me that I would arrive at my belief through my doubts. I was also asking other people questions, as by this time I was entertaining a lot in our home.

These constant questions annoyed Jim. He would tell me that I would ask people what kind of toothpaste they would use. The fact was, I didn't care about their private lives and I didn't want to know things that were none of my business. What I did want to know was what people thought about things and why they thought the way they did. I was surprised to find a lot of them didn't know why.

Now I recognized my problems in learning, but I was still afraid and upset much of the time. I knew it was necessary to deal with school people to get help for our four boys and dealing with them is enough to upset anyone. After being tutored, I would go to bed and when Jim came home I would say, "Don't ask me any questions that call for thinking."

He would fix dinner and leave me alone. Fortunately, this was happening less and less. I knew Jim didn't understand how reading could be so hard for anyone who had good intelligence to learn, and he had always believed me to be intelligent. But again, he said nothing and I was too tired to explain.

I would get up the next day ready to go back to tutoring. Of course, my housework went undone and I soon found that I also had to give up my church work. I had to cut back on everything so I could turn all my energy to learning for myself and getting help for the boys.

Jean had seen each of the boys and learned that all of them had severe reading problems. It was very clear that even with the progress that Jimmy was making, he would not be ready for sixth grade work in the fall. Without more help he could not manage in junior high school the following year.

Jean was a very loving person and felt badly when she thought about the boys having to go through what I had gone through. She called the psychologist to ask whether the school system had any kind of special class that would answer the boys' needs. Jimmy's teacher thought this was a good idea. Jimmy and Mark needed help most quickly, and perhaps for a longer time than Paul or John. We could not pay for tutoring for more than one, and even if we could, Jean could not take all five of us.

A conference was held at the school with the principal, the teachers of the two oldest boys, the psychologist, a representative from Special Education, Jean and me. Little did I know, this was to be the first of many conferences. Something had to be done for all four boys. It was not going to be easy, for the school was small and had no remedial reading teacher or special class. At that time reading problems were not being taken seriously by educators, so it was an uphill battle from the start.

Everyone agreed that Mark should have an intelligence test as soon as possible. They felt he might have a learning problem that might show up on the IQ test. His teacher liked him, and knew him to be a bright boy; they couldn't understand why he was having such a hard time with his work.

The teachers felt that a Special Education class was best for Jimmy and Mark, but thought they should be placed in separate classes. Jean said this would make it possible for us to arrange tutoring for Paul, while John could repeat the second grade and have tutoring the following year. The school didn't want John to repeat, but I pointed out his December birth date, his immaturity, and his almost total lack of skills for reading, writing and spelling.

Repeating the second grade was also a way of "buying time" until Jean could help Paul first, now in the third grade, and then John, before he was hopelessly far behind. This plan was so simple I felt good about it. I agreed on the condition that Jimmy and Mark would be placed in separate classes with children who had similar abilities and problems. The woman from Special Education said this would be done. By now I knew the longer this problem went on without correction, the worse it would become.

Jean and I were invited to visit four possible classes. We did so, and two teachers in two different schools seemed by far the best for the boys. They were both using methods similar to those that Jean had been using with Jimmy and me. They didn't apply them in just the same way, but the needed help was there in the classroom. One was a catch-up class and the other was for the Educable Mentally Retarded.

The name of this class bothered me, but the students in the class were just like any other kids, struggling to learn the basics. I wasn't completely happy, but couldn't put a finger on my uneasiness. The teachers were friendly enough, but some of the things that were said during our observation told me that even though the teachers had the right materials, they might not understand how to teach children who had these kinds of problems.

The teacher in the catch-up class seemed best to me, though I felt uneasy when, as she was talking to us, she made the statement, "I take my students into cursive as soon as possible, because you cannot reverse letters when you write in cursive."

I answered, "Oh yes you can!" Jean laughed and explained that I had this problem and that I was one of her students. The teacher looked at me dumfounded and went on as if it had never been said. I left, looking forward to Jimmy and Mark attending that class, in spite of my uneasy feelings in some areas.

Weeks passed, and not a word came from Pupil Personnel about the test for Mark. It was May and he would be in the fifth grade in the fall. I knew he couldn't do the work, and if there were no test, there would be no help. I was getting very worried about the whole thing. Every time I looked at my boys, fear came over me. I knew I couldn't let it stop me because I had to do something for the boys. The school still didn't want John to repeat, but I insisted.

I made calls to the supervisor of Pupil Personnel though I had great difficulty reaching him. Two of my calls were not returned. I had the growing feeling that I was going to have to go over his head for help. When I finally did talk to him, I had decided I would go to the Director of Pupil Personnel for help, because Jean had told me he was the one I had to see.

I was scared to death of these people, but knew it was up to me to fight for the boys. Jean would get information if I asked, but she was slow to push me into action. She knew what I was up against. I felt she was afraid I could not handle dealing with the school system, that it would finish me for good.

Nevertheless, I knew this was my fight, and I had to fight it as long as I could. From the beginnings of my dealings with the school, I could tell there was little or no understanding of this problem that I had lived with for so long, and I knew they didn't understand my boys' needs.

I knew nothing about education and how educators functioned. I had to find out for myself, and I soon learned that no one in the system was in any hurry to help me. When I had taught art, I had seen the boys' teachers every week and they urged me over and over to "do something," even if I had to go to the school board. But I couldn't "do something" if I didn't know what to do. Jimmy's teacher told Jean and me that she had only two students, in her class of 16, continue on grade level. She also told Jean, when I wasn't there, that she had encouraged me to do something about my children, because she knew I would.

That school year passed with all the teachers working as hard as they knew how, and with all of us waiting for help for Mark. It is very unusual for a family to get all good teachers at the same time, as we did at that school. I wish all the educators that we were to deal with later had been as nice, as kind and understanding as they tried to be.

Too often I didn't understand what educators were trying to say, or if they were really saying anything. They used words that I had never heard in my life. They seemed to use so many words to say nothing. I was surprised that even though the teachers wanted to help my boys, they didn't seem to understand how much Jean knew about learning problems and they didn't seem to want her advice. Sometime later, I asked Jean if it was my imagination, or if there was a lot of professional jealousy in these people. "You noticed!" she answered.

"Are you telling me that if the school has to get help from you or other educators outside of the school system who know about teaching children with learning disabilities, if it came to that, the school would not help? If I don't keep fighting, my boys will never learn to read? Is that what you are saying?"

Jean put her head down and said, "I don't know." I was shocked and felt helpless as I thought about it, but I knew from the start that if I was going to get help it would come from God, and I just knew that He would not let my boys be illiterate.

Chapter 7
Schools and Psychologists

It was June 1969, when I got an appointment to see the Director of Pupil Personnel Services. I asked Jean to go with me, thinking she could shed light on the problem. My four boys, Jean and I waited in a small room that had nothing but reading materials, which only Jean could read, to keep the boys busy. The Director saw each boy alone for testing which took less than an hour for all four. Then he saw Jean and me for about fifteen minutes.

He didn't describe his testing to us and he didn't ask any questions about the tutoring. Although he had known Jean would be with me, he seemed upset by it and went out of his way to be rude with her. He told me that the tutoring cost money, and "We (referring to Jean) don't mind spending your money."

He said that John and Mark were hyperactive, although the psychologist had not said Mark was. Mark was very active at home, but John was downright docile. I wondered how he could expect the boys to do well in the tests after they had been sitting uneasily, waiting to see him. He judged that the four boys had only "average intelligence," but said probably only John could be helped in a Special Education class. He didn't say why this was true.

I was so confused and upset I didn't think to ask him to explain his reason. I could not believe what was happening. Jean was so shaken by his rudeness that she said very little. He went on to say that reading and spelling are not all that important, and that I was a good example of this. He ended the conference quickly and said I would be hearing from him.

As we left the conference, I was just sick. I was so discouraged, and very offended. I asked Jean what he had against her. She said she didn't know, as she had never met him before. She told me she had never been so professionally mistreated in her career.

It was days before I could tell Jim about the meeting. He is an incurable optimist, and when I did tell him, he said he was sure the school system knew what they were doing. "I hope you are right," I answered. But I didn't think so.

Much to my surprise, I received a call about ten days later informing me that all four boys were to go to Poolesville Elementary School in the fall, since the classes would be restructured to include children who had problems similar to my boys' problems. Jimmy, Paul and Mark were to be in Special Education classes. John, the youngest, would repeat the second grade in a regular class. Psychological testing was done with Paul and John later in the summer. Now I was thinking that Jim's optimism about the school system was right. The boys and I relaxed for the summer.

Relaxed, what a joke! John broke his arm, and Mark and Jimmy had an accident while riding double on a bike.

I, too, added to the fun with one of my many decorating projects. We had a small, old, faded chair, so I decided to take the color out of the fabric. I took the chair outside and washed it down with bleach. I didn't know that bleach would burn on the skin, but I would soon found that out the hard way. I walked the floor day and night with pain. I was too ashamed to go to the doctor or tell anyone. I didn't want them to know I was that stupid.

A week before school started I called the psychologist and asked if I could take the boys to meet their teachers and to introduce them to their new school. The psychologist said she would meet me there. At the school I learned that the class that Jimmy, Paul and Mark would be in would have the teacher whose class I had visited before. She talked more on what she knew about this kind of problem.

When I asked if the classes had been restructured, she said they had not been changed; they were the same as last year. By this time I had come to the conclusion, after talking with others, that Special Education was a catchall for all kinds of problems. I decided to wait it out.

A day or two before school opened, the psychologist called to tell me the boys should stay at Edward Taylor School, where they had gone last year, because transportation was still being arranged. When I told my friends who were in the education field, one of them suggested that I drive the boys to Poolesville, because if I didn't, the boys would lose their space and the class would be full for the year.

On the opening day of school, Jim and I drove the boys to Poolesville. The principal told us they did not have authorization for the boys to be in that school. He said we could leave them and he would get the authorization from the central office. The next day when I took the boys, the principal said he had gotten authorization and that the boys were welcome. When partial transportation was worked out a few days later, I had to drive the boys five miles to meet the bus and pick them up in the afternoon.

Day after day I waited to see what would happen. I didn't like the classes, though Jimmy and Mark's teacher seemed good. But Jimmy and Mark were not happy, and they fought with each other, as they had never done before. Other school children would make fun of those in the special classes, and my boys didn't like it. Mark would not take it, he fought back. Jimmy didn't say anything.

I didn't know what to do. I knew they needed special help, which I couldn't give them, and even this class seemed better than nothing. But Paul was a different story. I was afraid he was losing all he had learned. The class seemed a waste of time for him.

I tried many ways to keep from worrying. One day when I was at home, I had received a sample envelope in the mail. I though my reading had improved to the point where I could read one of the words on the package: SOUP. I was hungry so I thought I'd try it. Laboring over the instructions I read "Mix with water," so I heated a cup of water and poured the contents of the envelope into it, put it in a bowl and sat down to eat it. The first bite was just awful and I knew there was something wrong. I picked up the envelope and noticed the first word started with a "W" and the third word I sounded out "MIX." I then realized that instead of SOUP I had Whiskey SOUR MIX.

Early in December, Jim and I were called to a conference at school. In addition to us, there were seven people from the school system. At this conference, another psychologist, one for Special Education, warned us that the placement for the boys could be damaging. It was true that Jimmy and Mark were not getting along as they had before, and were not as happy as they used to be. I also feared that Paul was falling farther behind.

We asked what help the boys could have in place of these classes. We tried to explain that if we had only one child with the problem, we could pay for care outside the school system, but since there were four children, we couldn't afford it.

The truth was even if we had had the money, there was no one in the area close to us trained to teach them. Jean had all the students she could tutor, and a waiting list besides. Then the principal said that they had other children with problems in learning, which were far more serious than our boys'.

I said that I couldn't take other children's problems on my shoulders, even though I would like to. I had all I could do to take care of my own children. The room became very quiet.

In that conference we finally agreed that the boys would be placed in regular classes immediately with added help by the Special Education Teacher and Remedial Reading Teacher. The Remedial Reading Teacher did not want to take the boys at all because she said her classes were too full already. We were told that in addition, the Special Education Teacher would work with the boys and the Remedial Reading Teacher would give the boys extra help outside their regular classes.

After Christmas vacation, in January 1970, Jimmy, Mark and Paul were taken from their Special Education classes and placed in regular classes at Poolesville, with additional help promised for the Remedial Reading Teacher. Jimmy repeated the fifth grade, which Mark was in, and Paul repeated the third grade. Mark's problem was as serious as Jimmy's and more so than Paul's. It was never explained why he should not repeat his grade, as the other boys were doing, until I asked why. The principal said he placed them that way to provide the best teachers for them.

I knew I was up against the wall and had to do something fast. That Sunday in church I was walking by the chapel and saw a friend sitting alone. She worked on Capitol Hill for, then Congressman, Gerald Ford. I looked at her and thought maybe she could help. I went into the chapel, sat down beside her and told her the whole story.

She was surprised and said she would see what she could do. It was obvious to her that I was very upset. She said she had a friend who worked on the

Education Committee. She called me the next day and said they had called the State Education Office and asked them to look into the problem. She called me later to tell me that the school system said they were doing all they could. A written report had been asked for and when I asked for a copy, she said she would try to get one for me. I never got it.

By now my vocabulary was growing. When Jim and I got into an argument, I could take his four syllable words and turn them into street language in no time flat. Now he told me I had a tongue like a snake, that I had a way of separating the wheat from the chaff.

As I listened to the educators talk, using terms like "task oriented," and "perceptual motor skills," I promised myself that no matter how much my vocabulary increased, and if I ever learned what they were talking about, I would never learn education jargon. Educators talk to all kinds of people, I thought, not just to each other. It seemed to me they were hiding behind their big words.

I went to most of the meetings alone, still believing it was my fight. Jim didn't really understand and I didn't expect him to. If educators didn't understand, how could he? I knew that if I needed him, he would be there. By now even Jim was beginning to see how hopeless it all was. When I felt the educators weren't taking me seriously because I was an illiterate housewife and mother, I would ask Jim for help. He could be very firm and they indeed took him seriously.

In time, both of us became more concerned and worried about the boys and their classes, because we could not see how they were going to overcome their learning problems with the present set-up in regular classes.

Even this plan of extra help by the Special Education and Remedial Reading teachers was quickly dropped. After January, the boys no longer had anything to do with Special Education. The truth was that the Special Education teacher knew the symptoms of the problem, but she didn't know how to teach the problem. She knew they needed phonics with a lot of repetition. But Paul's teacher and the other classroom teachers, and even the Remedial Reading teacher, didn't realize this. I knew that if the boys got a strong foundation in reading, they could build on it and learn words over the years. Even though they would still have a hard time with reading and spelling, they would not be illiterate. After they got away from the pressure of being flooded with reading and writing of words, they could improve their skills.

I knew from my own experience that the remedial reading help the boys were getting was not concentrated enough, and the classroom work in reading was not coordinated with it. Because the classroom teachers did not truly understand the nature of the problem, there instances of homework material the boys could not read and a scolding for "not trying" on a spelling test.

I was bothered, too, by the programmed book the boys brought home from school for the remedial class, because it was little more than practice in matching. This material did not help to train their ears and eyes to know the difference between words like "want" and "went" and "ever" and "even" in their reading. Also, Jimmy and Mark remained together for remedial help, and this still caused enough conflict to interfere with learning.

More conferences followed. We had gone from dealing with people in the school system, to the state and Federal Government. Jim was in a weekly Bible Study with Congressman L.H. Fountain. He called him at his office and told him of the problem, asking if he could help. Jean, Jim and I went to Capitol Hill, and his office called NIH to see if any help was available. The people at NIH said they give money to the states, and it filters down to the family.

There really was no help to be had, though no one would come right out and say; "We don't know how to help your children."

Out of all the school officials we had contact with, there was one man, a pupil services worker, who was really concerned. He would talk to me as much as he could, and anytime that I called him, he not only listened, but he heard what I said.

One day he told me, "Mrs. Howell, I tried to tell the others that they had to be direct with you. I said, 'You can't fool her; she knows what she is talking about.'" I loved him and he will never know how much I appreciated him, but he had no authority to really do anything about the problem. All he could do is say what he thought.

Report cards made me weary over the years. It was not the grades, which I could understand, but the statements, comments and questions from the school people. They would ask me what time the boys went to bed, if they got enough rest. (They went to bed between 8:00 and 9:00 every night. TV watching was limited.) School people were reluctant to ask too many questions about the home life because I did not appreciate them, and I knew that this was a teaching problem which home life had nothing to do with. It was my feeling that children go to school over twelve years, or until they are sixteen, six hours a day, five days a week, nine months a year. How can it be the home's fault if children don't learn to read? The home is not a classroom.

The school would say that the boys needed to practice reading at home. I wondered how, since they couldn't read, they were expected to practice. Jim left for work at 6:00 a.m. and he returned home at 7:00 p.m. I was unable to help them, because reading was still very hard and tiring for me. I could not face it at four in the afternoon, even though I tried. My own frustration, when dealing with words, added to the boys' frustration, was proving to be too much for us. They needed help from someone who was not going through the same thing.

The teachers told me the boys were trying hard, though the report cards reflected poor work habits. I could not understand that. They were flooded with a sea of reading and writing material and none of it made sense. Of course they had poor work habits.

A woman from a local paper who had heard about us through Jean and others called one day and asked if she could write an article about the boys and me. Several thoughts went through my mind: it might help me get the school system to help the boys and other students who were not learning how to read. By now, I knew if I had had the right teaching early in my schooling, I would not be so low in reading and spelling. I might not have been college material, but at least I would know how to read and spell well enough to get along in life. So I said 'yes' to the woman who wanted to write the article.

After the article was printed, I found myself talking to people all the time about the teaching of reading. They wanted help and I couldn't help them. I did what I could, referring them to Jean or someone else, encouraging them to request psychological testing so they could get help from the school. The testing itself seemed a waste of time to me. I couldn't see the good of it. All it did was tell me my boys had problems in learning and especially in reading and writing. I already knew that. But the educators took comfort in tests. Eventually it became apparent to me that the boys were being very upset by tests. It seemed to me it would make much more sense to teach them. I recommended psychological testing for other parents only because without it, there would be no help from the school system.

It made me feel bad that I couldn't help those who needed help so badly. I knew the only thing that could help people with learning problems was the right kind of teaching. It had taken me years to find that for myself. I told people about Kingsbury Center where Jean tutored. It was the only place I knew of where they might get some help.

It was May when Jimmy was sent home with a punishment assignment for missing 32 out of 37 spelling words on a test. The words all had more than one syllable, and many were proper names, such as Tallahassee, Montpelier and Olympia. He could not even read words, such as education and examination, which were on the list. He was to write the 32 misspelled words 50 times each.

Jimmy was quiet and extremely intelligent. If he felt angry about the assignment, it seemed to me that he didn't show it. He liked the teacher and wanted to please him. Although he didn't want to tackle this assignment, he sat down and started to work.

After Jimmy had been at work for three and a half hours, Jim stopped him. At the rate Jimmy was working, he estimated it would take him 16 hours, working steadily, to complete the assignment. Jim sent a note to the teacher saying that Jimmy had spent a lot of time on the assignment, but questioned whether this kind of practice would really help him, in the end, learn to spell.

Jimmy told us his teacher read the note and told his class that one boy's family had complained about the assignment. He also added that everybody in the room, who was not as smart as Jimmy, was dyslexic. He said the assignment was ridiculous, but so was missing 32 words. Jimmy hated to be humiliated and as he told us about the reading of the note, it was obvious how bad he felt.

I was worried about the possible ill effects of this kind of assignment on Jimmy, and asked Jean to call the teacher and explain how hard it was for

Jimmy to do this kind of assignment. She had had to work with Jimmy in the beginning to get him to see reading and spelling as tasks he could do with the right kind of training.

In this phone conversation the teacher dismissed Jimmy's disability and then declared it was time everyone stopped "coddling him." He told Jean that even though Jimmy was not too smart, he believed he was able to copy the assigned spelling words. He insisted that an assignment of 1600 words was "a light assignment" for a fifth grader, even if it took 16 hours to complete. He told Jean that if Jimmy's parents did not permit him to complete the assignment at home, he would see to it that he finished it at school.

At this time, Jimmy was reading on about a third-grade level, according to the Remedial Reading teacher. Jean was so shocked she could only tell the teacher she was just trying to be helpful.

There was a growing feeling from the area office and the Poolesville administration that the boys should be returned to Taylor School, even though there was no special help of any kind, not even a reading teacher. I was back where I started. I had had it.

At this point, I asked a group of friends to help summarize our experiences in writing, so we could send a letter to the Superintendent of Schools to plead for help. When that 18-page letter was written, in June of 1970, I sent copies to the seven members of the Board of Education. Even though it was 18 pages, I didn't put everything that had happened into the letter, for I thought the Superintendent would call or ask me to come in, and I could then tell him everything.

There was no direct reply from either the Superintendent of any of the Board members. But the effect of the letter was felt almost overnight. We received a phone call from the area office and Jim, Jean and I were asked to come to a meeting that week. Those present were: the Area Director, Supervisor of English and Language Arts, Supervisor of Pupil Services, Pupil Personnel Worker, Remedial Reading Teacher, the Principal from Taylor, the Principal from Poolesville and a Psychologist.

They took two and a half hours to tell us they didn't know what they were going to do, except that the boys were going to be returned to Taylor School in the fall. They would also try to assign a part-time reading teacher there. I just felt now they would teach my boys to read.

In the 18-page letter, I had told the Superintendent that I would call for an appointment in two weeks to discuss the letter with him, and that I would bring a friend who had his Doctorate in Education. When I did call, in two weeks, his secretary would not give me an appointment. I told Jim, and he called, but he could not get an appointment either. Instead, the secretary connected him with the Administrative Assistant, who told Jim they were doing a study about children with learning problems and they couldn't tell us anything until the study was completed. Jim asked when the study would be ready and was told in July. Jim asked for a copy and was promised he would get one. We never received it.

By now, Jim was used to living with the problems the boys and I were having. He didn't like the thought of having a wife who was illiterate, but he could live with it. He also didn't like seeing me in so much pain. When he would play golf on the weekends, he would take the boys with him and I could stay home by myself. I liked to be alone most of the time now.

Jim had never seen me cry before; not even when mother died. But when I was alone, I cried a lot. I didn't want anyone else to know, but Jim and the boys could tell. I always felt so alone, even though I had friends who let me know they would help if I needed it. Dr. and Mrs. Clews and Mary were always there.

I prayed a lot, though I didn't know what kind of God I was praying to. But no matter what was happening, He was always there, as quiet as grass growing, and just as certain. When I came to what I thought was the end of myself, He knew I could go much farther. When I felt completely helpless, He was always there waiting to help me with a word or two of encouragement or a feeling of love that only He could give.

I would fight with Him constantly. "Why, God, why?" was the question that I always asked. Why would anyone do this to a person? Even though I have learned more and grown closer to Him, I have never had this "why?" answered.

Chapter 8
Music

That summer of 1970, after trying to battle the school system for my boys, Jean told us about Talking Books. These records are for persons unable to read printed books, and may be borrowed free of charge from libraries carrying materials for the blind and physically handicapped.

For a long time, it was hard for me to listen to someone read, and my mind would wander. However, I did like to hear Jim Nabors sing and I thought I would train myself by listening to his songs. I have always had trouble memorizing words of songs unless I sing them over and over, and even then, I usually can't retain them for long.

My Jim tells me to this day there is not a song written that I know two lines to. He once said he didn't think I knew the National Anthem.

I answered, "Oh, yes I do. Oh say, can you see, any bedbugs on me. If you do, take a few, and pound them black and blue."

He put his arms around me and said, "Dolly, that's not the National Anthem." I told him it was as far as I was concerned. It was nice that he could laugh about my problem.

Jim bought me all of Jim Nabors' albums, including "The Lord's Prayer." I would listen to them almost every day for hours. I picked out three songs that I liked best, and then tried to memorize the words as he sang. Jim Nabors has a clear, strong, pleasant voice and I could understand almost all the words.

But no matter how hard I tried, I couldn't memorize all of them. It was very frustrating. I even wrote down the words as he sang. But it did little good. On one of his songs, which I especially liked, I couldn't understand why Jim Nabors was saying, "How great Thou aren't" until I asked Jim.

He laughed and said, "'Art,' Dolly, not 'aren't.'"

I listened to Jim Nabors sing so much that my Jim teased me that I was being foolish about him. I wasn't, but I did like to hear him sing. I liked to hear some other singers, too, but I hated rock and roll. I disliked it so much I wouldn't allow it in my house. If the boys wanted to hear it, they had to play it in the basement, keeping it low. Needless to say, we fought a lot.

One day as I was listening to Jim Nabors sing, I thought I heard him sing a word wrong. I always had a hard time hearing when someone was saying a word wrong on purpose, as in jokes or on TV, so I thought I wasn't understanding it right. My Jim came into the room and I asked him what Jim Nabors was singing.

"Help me make it through the night," he answered.

"No," I said, "that can't be." I played it again, and there it was, "Hep me make it through the night," and I had heard it right. I was so amused.

Jim laughed and said, "My grandmother used to say 'hep' for 'help.' "

It was only later that I realized how the words of the song were planted in my mind. I discovered something else during the listening period. One day, as I walked to the record player, I put my hand on the speaker. The song was "I Can't Stop Loving You." I could feel the beat of the drum. The music was so real it scared me and I pulled my hand away quickly. It was the first time I heard or felt the background music distinguished from the singer. It was all lumped together before. Now I had three distinct sounds: the background music, the words and his voice. Later, I found earphones brought it even closer and I could enjoy the music without interference.

For a long time after feeling the speaker vibrate. I was afraid to place my hand on the speaker again, but when I finally did, the music came alive and I began to put my hands on the speaker all the time. One day when John, then 9, was in the room as I was listening to the "Hallelujah Chorus" from Handel's "*MESSIAH*," I asked him to put his hand on the speaker.

He stood, feeling the vibration and listening to the music for a few moments, he went out to play. About two hours later, he came back into the kitchen and said, "Mom, I can't get that music out of my mind."

I listened to Jim Nabors for about two years, then tried opera and classical music. Later, my sister Betty gave me a record on "How to Speak Spanish" and I thought I would try to learn that language. After listening to this record many times, I tried to speak Spanish with Jim laughing at me. So I decided to forget about speaking Spanish. Jean wrapped it up by saying I was having enough trouble with English, without trying another language.

I was also listening to the Talking Books longer and longer at a time. Among my first were Dante's *INFERNO*, Milton's *PARDISE LOST*, And *THE RISE AND FALL OF THE THIRD REICH*, which was 34 records. At the end of those 34 records, although I learned many things, I couldn't remember any names and dates, except those I already knew.

When the boys were not being tutored that summer, we would go swimming, and while they swam, I tried to read Plato, *THE PASSIONATE STATE OF MIND*, by Eric Hoffer, and the Bible. They all had one thing in common: one sentence held a whole lot. I read the Bible because I still wanted to know about God. I was full of questions and confusion about what He was like. I didn't want to know what other people thought about Him. I wanted to know from the Bible. To deal with so much frustration as I had, and to feel so lacking and stupid, made me question what the love of God was.

The discipline in trying to read the Bible came in handy, for by this time I was reading on a controlled level of fourth grade in tutoring, and an independent level of late second or early third grade.

I would work on a paragraph for a long time and found that very rewarding. I will never forget the following quotation from Plato:

> "No one will love that which gives pain, and in which after much toil he makes little progress. And again, if he is forgetful and retains nothing of what he learns, will he not be an empty vessel? Laboring in vain, he must end in hating himself and his fruitless occupation."

After Jean started tutoring me, I began to write. The thoughts and feelings of all the years up to then began to take form in words. I wrote the way I talked, and it was a real mess, because my sentence structure and paragraphing were poor, and most of the time I misspelled words, or left them out entirely.

Jean would try to help me and she was so kind about it that I kept on. At one point I wrote, "I reached out my hand into an ocean of promises, laid down by the educators of my society, and pulled it back to find nothing but water sifting through my fingers."

Jim would also help me with my writing, correcting my sentences and punctuation. He would spell words for me, but he would call the letters out too fast and frustrate me to no end. I would get very upset and confused, and yell at him. So he would spell the words over many times, each time slower. After a while, my yelling didn't seem to bother him – about spelling, that is.

I would call Mary any time and ask her to spell the simplest words for me. She didn't seem to mind.

One day, I found a book of poems at home. I went through it and found *NOT AS I WILL* by Helen Hunt Jackson, which I thought was an easy poem to read; it wasn't. I could read most of the words, but couldn't make sense of the way the lines went, and had trouble with the confusion of rhyming words. Later Jim read the poem to me and I went over it so much that I memorized the first two verses. Later I wrote this poem:

GRADUATION DAY

It was quite an achievement for me,
Because you see, a scholar I will never be.
I had no honors given me,
Just a piece of paper.

That would insure some happiness and a new life,
All just for me.
I look ahead to tomorrow with great joy
And happiness to be free.

When I looked back, there was no happiness to see.
Just a cloud of confusion and loneliness
That was always around me.
Funny cloud, no one could see it but me.

The Principal called my name that night.
I walked forward with great delight.
Great golden wings he handed me.

For a moment I wondered if that cloud would go with me.
But that couldn't be.
I was free.
A new life was waiting for me.

As the years went by, I could see those wings
Would not fly with me.
Why did he give them to me?

I would not have longed for that new life;
I would have known I could not be free.
Disappointment has always been part of me.
That is not so bad, you see.

But that cloud, that cloud,
It came with me.

Then I began to write children's stories with a vocabulary on about a third grade level. I couldn't understand where the thoughts were coming from, until I was talking with a friend about my writing, and the words came to me, "This time, Lord, You gave me a mountain." I knew the words and thoughts were coming from the music I listened to. From then on, when I wanted to write, I would listen to Jim Nabors sing until I found a thought on which to build a story.

Out of all the stories I wrote, the one I liked best was the one about the life of an apple. I couldn't get the words, "Life travels in a circle, first there is laughter, then there is tears," out of my mind until I wrote the apple story.

Jean asked me to write for my high school transcript. So I did the next best thing and asked Jim to write for it. After I received it and saw that they had recorded an IQ of 69 (retarded), I wrote back to ask how they had arrived at such a figure. I received the following letter:

Dear Mrs. Howell:

In reply to your request for information concerning the types of tests, which had been administered to you while you were in high school, I am offering you the following information:

Type of test: This was the California Test of Mental Maturity, which was given to all students in certain grades during their school career.

The tests were conducted by each teacher and hand scored locally.

I personally looked over your entire record and found other tests, which placed you in the average range of intelligence. If the test score given has created some problem for you, I would be glad to send other information; however, if it is only for your own satisfaction, this will no doubt suffice. Your other tests indicate you are of average intelligence, in a range similar to most students tested.

Jim wrote back and asked for more information and received the following letter:

Our test records for students at the time of your graduation are rather meager. What we have on the Otis Printer-Cunningham, Stanford Achievement and Iowa have on the various test grades, 1 through 12, show you to be within the average ability. However, your grades are a good "D" average. You did take several good academic subjects.

Good academic subjects were required! I had to take them. Why, I wondered, did my transcript show an IQ of 69 if tests taken at the time showed me to be in the average range of ability? Also, what is good about a "D" average for three straight years? Why would they want to say that someone had an IQ of 69 if that wasn't right? I was very puzzled and upset over how insensitive they were, but I knew there was nothing I could do about it.

Before the summer ended, the PTA President from the Gaithersburg school where the boys had gone got in touch with me. He had read in the published article written about my experiences that the boys had attended the Gaithersburg school and he wanted to discuss our experiences there. Many of the parents were trying to remove the principal and he wanted more information.

In our discussion, he told me he had heard of a 20-page confidential file, being held by the school system, which was on me. I was surprised, and though I wanted to see it, I knew at that time parents couldn't read confidential files. I couldn't help but wonder what there was to be said about me that would take 20 pages.

Chapter 9
Here we go again

"Here we go again," I thought, as all four boys began the fall term at their neighborhood school, Edward Taylor. Talking Books hadn't worked for them; they didn't like them. Maybe it was because they lacked the discipline to sit and listen to them. TV may have spoiled them by offering something to watch at the same time. A reading specialist had been assigned to Taylor School that year, and she saw each of the boys three times a week for one half hour each time.

Because of my letter to the Superintendent, I was now known in the school system as a troublemaker. The pupil service worker told me, "I will be perfectly honest with you, Mrs. Howell. I have been in meetings where they spoke unkindly about you. I told them they didn't know you, and all I got was into trouble myself."

One of the new teachers at Taylor School who had never even met me told one of my neighbors that I was a nice person, but I ran "dyslexia" into the ground. I told my neighbor the teacher was wrong, I wasn't the least bit nice.

At first I thought the feelings against me didn't matter. I couldn't see how all the educators in the world could do any more to me than they already had. I had the feeling that I could tell some of them that their teaching was wrong and they would agree, but to prove them wrong made them really angry with me.

Some educators in our school system would insist that my children were not dyslexic or learning disabled, yet they would not say why the boys were not learning to read and write as they should. I knew what they were thinking: the boys were not learning because of me. But they would not say that, at least not to me. One person even told me there was no such thing as dyslexia. At that time, most educators believed that learning problems were caused by emotional problems or low IQ, and they knew the boys didn't have low IQ's.

However, I liked the new principal at Taylor, and tried to work with her. Jimmy was now in sixth grade and Mark was repeating the fifth. Paul was a fourth grader and John was in the third grade.

Another year and a lot more conferences followed. I was feeling a little better about the boys, the school, and the school system. I hoped that at last they would teach the boys to read. I wasn't counting on it, though. I worked as a volunteer in the school, and found the principal very considerate of me. I wondered how it would be the following year with a new principal and a new reading specialist.

During that year, I found out about the Seventh Day Adventist School. My sister, Norma, had pulled her two children out of public school. Because she was a member of the Seventh Day Adventist church, she put her children in their school. Because her son had had trouble reading while he was in public school, I offered to go to the Seventh Day Adventist School and explain the family history of learning problems.

The school had about forty children in grades one through eight. There were three teachers. One of them, Betty Ullrich, was worried about her own son's reading. She was a kind and very warm person. She had read to her son, George, since he was one year old, and there was no TV in the home to blame his problems on. He had repeated the first grade, and at the age of 11, he was still not able to read or spell well.

A few years ago, I would never have believed anyone who told me I would be able to help others with reading. In my mind it would have been impossible. Yet weak as I was in reading, I thought maybe I could help George, as there was no one else to suggest. Jean still had a waiting list. When a friend asked me what gave me the courage to offer help, I said, "When God says so, you go."

George was up to go into fifth grade in the fall. When I began working with him that summer, he couldn't do first-grade reading work. I began with him as Jean had begun with me, training him to hear short vowel sounds and blends, and sounding out words. I still couldn't do sight words at that point, so I got the words from Jean, made cards with the words to be sounded out, and George and I struggled along together.

Jean didn't say a word about the fact that I was doing this. In looking back on it, I can see how important my tutoring George was for helping me to retain what I was learning from Jean. I knew at the end of the summer that George still needed more help than I had given him so far.

Since we had decided to send Jimmy to the Seventh Day Adventist School so he wouldn't fall further behind, I offered to stay at the school and work with George and others who needed help. Mrs. Ulrich asked the principal if I could tutor as a volunteer, and of course he wanted to see me. I was afraid of the questions he might ask, since he knew of my problems with reading and spelling. After we talked, he said he would be glad for me to work at the school.

I tutored every afternoon, using the materials I had made, since that was all I had. I didn't feel confident being a tutor, yet the need was so great I couldn't do anything else. "How could I," I wondered, "have dared help others?" Yet I knew that what little I could teach was more than they would get in the classroom, because they would soon fall far behind without the proper one-on-one tutoring.

By the end of that year, George was tested and found to read at a third grade level, and tested on twelfth grade level in math. As of this writing, he is in his first year of medical school.

Six weeks into the fall term that same year Mark came home from Taylor School very upset and said he didn't want to go back. He had been having trouble, and the boys had been told by me to try to understand

92

that the teachers didn't know much about their kind of problem, even though it was very common, and didn't always realize they were being unkind. But my boys knew that, if ever they couldn't stand it any longer, I would do something about it. Mark's teacher had been calling him names, half-jokingly, such as "idiot," "stupid" and "simple-minded fool," but Mark didn't find that so funny.

It had happened so often and upset him so much that I took him out of Taylor School and put him in the Seventh Day Adventist School with Jimmy, even though we couldn't afford it. I found out later that Mark wasn't the only one who had suffered from name calling by that teacher. The week after I took Mark out, report cards were given out and Mark's friends told him the teacher had read his grades to the class.

As the year went by, I found Mr. James Youngberg, the principal, and Mrs. Ullrich and Miss Berent, another teacher of the Seventh Day Adventist School, to be very loving people. The students accepted me as the reading teacher, and I would drill the first, second and third graders on sounds, every Monday. I had to watch myself very closely to use the right sounds with the letters. I didn't teach the short "e" and "i" as I got them mixed up, and couldn't hear them clearly.

Soon, Mr. Youngberg asked me to teach reading comprehension to the seventh and eighth graders once a week. I used *THE PASSIONATE STATE OF MIND* by Eric Hoffer because the sentences and paragraphs were short. I began to feel at home in school, and sometimes I would even cover for Miss Berent. The students would come to me and ask, "Mrs. Howell, how do you spell 'hungry'?"

I would answer, "I don't know."

"But Mrs. Howell, you're the reading teacher," they would tell me.

"I know, but I can't spell 'hungry'. Go look it up or ask Mrs. Ullrich." I would always see to it that the child spelled the word right.

Sometimes while I was tutoring, I would go to Mrs. Ullrich or Mr. Youngberg and ask, "What is this word?" I often needed help with reading and spelling and felt free to ask even parents who were working at the school as volunteers.

It seemed strange to me to be working in a school and feel so free, and to be treated with such respect and loving kindness. We were always laughing with one another and I never knew what was going to happen next. One time I was looking out the window and saw a small animal. I asked my student, "What is that?" He let out a scream, "Possum," and the entire seventh and eighth grade ran out the front door, pushing me up against the wall, with Mr. Youngberg running ahead of them. I learned then that they loved animals and wanted to see the possum up close.

I knew the parents must have worried about someone who couldn't read or write well, teaching their children to read. Yet we could all see improvement in the children. One of the parents who was a volunteer that worked with me, told me one day that her husband asked her how I could tutor when I couldn't read very well. She told him, "She just does. You'd have to watch her to understand it."

I was tutoring her daughter and she was very pleased because the daughter had had so much trouble with reading and spelling in the past. In later years her daughter began to write lovely poetry. Sadly, I was not that much help to her son, who was three years older. He had repeated first and second grades. The earlier a child's learning disability is recognized and treated, the more chance they have for success.

On one occasion, several of the boys caught a black snake on the school playground. It was as big as a car - to me, anyway. Mrs. Ullrich told me not to let the kids know that I was afraid of that snake or they would use it.

At lunchtime, I was walking down the hall when the boys came towards me. George had the snake around his neck and its head lying on his shoulder. They were going to pass me and go out the front door. As they came toward me, I kept looking at the head of the snake and telling myself not to let them know I was afraid of that snake. The closer they got, the more afraid I got. Finally, I stopped in my tracks, and started walking backwards.

George saw that I was afraid and started towards me, holding that snake's head out in front of him. I let out a scream that you could have heard in New York City. Mrs. Ullrich came running and I was running the other way. She stopped the boys and let them know, "If you scare Mrs. Howell with that snake again, I will turn it loose." Although they were tempted many times, they wanted the snake more than they wanted to scare me and they knew Mrs. Ullrich always kept her word.

Meanwhile, a new assistant superintendent in our public school system told Jean that children could no longer be released for tutoring during school hours. That really took me by surprise. I knew the chance I was taking in fighting a big system like ours, but somehow I didn't think it would affect Jean, or my children. I had a feeling this was happening because of the letter I had sent to the superintendent asking for help. Fortunately, the parents of children Jean was tutoring, as well as the Citizen's Committee for Reading, that I was a member of, fought this decision successfully. High administrators in the system overruled the decision and the children again were released to Jean for tutoring during school hours.

Paul was doing well and seemed to be overcoming his problem, but John was doing badly in everything except reading, in which he was doing a little better.

Meanwhile, Mary asked me to help her son Patrick with math. I asked Betty Ullrich to help me so that I could help him, and found that in adding and subtracting, I was regrouping from left to right. After I got that straightened out, I helped Patrick for a while and then I decided, in desperation, to try to help John, who was learning so little in school. It seemed to me that he was a marked child and his teachers didn't want to put too much effort into teaching him. The truth is they probably didn't know what to do with him.

Jimmy and Mark were doing much better in the Seventh Day Adventist School and were very happy there. Jimmy's teacher was Mr. Youngberg, and Mark's teacher was Mrs. Ullrich. These teachers were very sympathetic to their problem and did all they could to help the boys. I found them to be the best classroom teachers I had ever known, although they had had no more training in this problem than any other teachers. One thing they did have was real caring and concern about the children and their futures.

Near the end of the school year, I was called to our public schools to talk about Paul and John. During the conference, I mentioned to the reading specialist and the principal, that each year, each reading teacher in turn would start the boys at a low level and bring them up to their so-called grade level. It was obvious to me that if they were really brought up to grade level at the end of each year, they wouldn't need to be started below grade level the following year.

The principal asked me why I thought this happened, and I answered, "My boys have a misunderstood problem that teachers no little about."

"What do you think your children's' problems are?" she asked.

"Dyslexia," I answered.

She then said, "We have children who have learning problems because of emotional problems, but in your case, I think you are right."

After talking a little more, I thanked them both and left with the hope that I would never again have to deal with the Montgomery County School System, for John and Paul were to join his two brothers at

Hadley Acres, the Seventh Day Adventist School. John had volunteered to repeat the fourth grade if he could go to the same school as his brothers and have Mrs. Ullrich, whom he loved, for his teacher. It was arranged that all four boys would go to Hadley Acres in September. Money was a problem, but it was the least of my worries; I knew it would come from somewhere.

Chapter 10
The Seventh Day Adventist School

At the time the newspaper article about me was published, the writer asked if she could write a book about me. She collected material from my files, talked to me, and seemed very interested in the project. After two years, when nothing resulted, I asked her for the material so I could do the book myself.

It was a good time for me to take another big step. The boys were happily settled in the Seventh Day Adventist School. Even though repeating a grade had been such a trauma for me, I could see now it was the best thing and was glad John was willing to repeat fourth grade. I continued there as a volunteer tutor, mostly for the first and second graders who needed extra help.

Though I never got the material back from the writer, I started this book without it. The struggle began, and I worked on it whenever I could. It became part of my life, like tutoring and other volunteer jobs, such as helping sell fresh Florida oranges and grapefruit at the school.

This job gave me a chance to learn to work with money. Mrs. Ullrich checked everything I did. The money part was easier for me than writing names and addresses on an order form. To this day, I can see and hear Mrs. Ullrich as she held one of those forms in her hand, saying, "I know who wrote this one." We would all laugh and she would change the spelling.

We laughed a lot at school. They got a kick out of the way I would say things. One day, things were so busy and confusing I said, "This place will make you lose your insanity." I also told some of the students that Washington was President during the Evolutionary War.

Even with the fun at times, and what seemed like a good beginning for that school year, things were changing. Part of the staff changed, including the principal and the enrollment had grown to 60 students. I was tutoring 19 of these children and even with my weakness in reading and spelling, I could see growth in the children I was tutoring.

One first grade boy would leave the school to go home at every opportunity. His teacher asked me to work with him just to keep him fully occupied. After two weeks, it became obvious to me that he was ready to begin to read. When I told the teacher, she said, "No, he needs to be taught reading readiness skills."

I couldn't convince her reading readiness was a waste of time for him. She let me know she was the teacher and I was the helper. About three days later, she came to me and said that she had been writing sentences on the blackboard for her third graders when she noticed this first grade boy had been reading each sentence aloud. She laughed about this and I asked her if I could teach him to read. She said yes.

Once the boy learned how words were put together, he learned to read without me. He also stopped running away from school. She was one of the many teachers who thought that her education gave her more knowledge of learning problems than my experience did.

I could help some students, but I knew many of them would not get the kind of tutoring help they needed. Some, like Betty Ullrich's son, George, were able to find a tutor through Jean. It felt good to get help for these children, but it was hard for me to see them get the help they needed and not be able to afford it for my own boys.

Paul and John were happy in school with Mrs. Ullrich as their teacher, but Jimmy and Mark were becoming more and more frustrated in the classroom. They were not interested in the long hours spent listening to religious lectures, though they did enjoy their classmates and the outdoor activities.

As the year went by, the classroom problems with the teacher became more and more upsetting, yet the idea of returning my sons to the public schools was unthinkable. The staff at the school was aware of the situation, and I decided to stay with the school, hoping things would improve.

My decision changed in January, when I developed a health problem and decided to quit my volunteer work and spend more time writing the book. Up to this point, Betty had helped me with it whenever she could, and when I showed Jean the first chapter, she liked it and told me to keep on. She said that my writing was very direct and clear. I still kept in touch with Jean, though I had stopped going to her for tutoring because I was so busy providing transportation and doing my volunteer work.

Though I made a decision to quit my volunteer work, it was not to be. One day, while I was tutoring, I noticed the principal watching me. Later he came to me and said, "You don't know how much we appreciate your working with these children. You are so patient with them."

I was surprised at this because no one had ever told me I was patient. When I told the principal I was quitting my volunteer work, we received our monthly tuition bill, with a letter telling me that the school appreciated my tutoring and we were to have one month tuition free. I was very pleased and told the principal how much I appreciated the letter. He said, "Every time I thought about those oranges coming in, and you not being here, I didn't know what we were going to do."

I was taken back and still planned to quit, but that didn't work out because the secretary was unable to work regularly. I ended up doing some of her work and the tutoring. That school would not let me go and plans for finishing the book had to wait until June.

Once summer came, I continued my volunteer tutoring in my home, and worked on the book. Jim had bought a typewriter for me and I typed the manuscript with the hunt and peck system.

It was 64 typewritten pages. Since I had never read anything but third grade books all the way through, I thought 64 pages, double-spaced, was a lot. Though Jean had taken a job with the Library of Congress, and moved to Washington, D.C., she was kind enough to edit the book for me. I called the book *I CLIMBED A MOUNTAIN* and sent it to Southern Publishing Association, which was a Seventh Day Adventist publisher.

Then I spent the summer tutoring, and tried to tutor John, but it seemed the emotional ties made the threat of failure very real. John didn't like to have me tutor him, so we quit.

I was continuing to learn on my own, as well as to tutor. They seemed to go together. I was getting better at short vowel sounds, but the difficulty was still there. Key sounds such as "ar" in car, "ir" in bird, "or" in sport, and "ur" in purse, were too hard for me to read. I got them mixed up. And I still couldn't teach sight words which fit no rules. Separated from the page, they were too confusing for me. So my tutoring was still just in reading, on a first and second grade level.

It was time to be thinking about Jimmy's school for the fall. He would be going into ninth grade, and if he wanted to continue in the Seventh Day Adventist School, he would have to go to the Academy in Hagerstown, which would mean he would have to board there. The school had a good reputation and a good staff, and after visiting it, we decided to send Jimmy there. The tuition was high, and I would have to find a job to help pay for it.

In September, when Jimmy started at the Academy, I tried to find a job. It was the second time since Jim and I got married that I had to apply for a job, and I dreaded it. Since I couldn't fill out a job application, Mary Shay went with me to the dime store where I was applying. When she noticed that I would have to take a test as well as make change, which I was not good at, I gave up that idea.

I heard about a job at the Seventh Day Adventist Nursing Home, and this time another friend went with me to help fill out the application. I got that job in the housecleaning department, which I hated.

It was boring, the employees were always gossiping, and our supervisor treated us with a little less respect than a cockroach. One instance of this was when Jim was to have eye surgery and I asked my supervisor for the day off. She told me that I should schedule surgery after work. I went to the woman in charge, explained the problem to her, and she told me to take the day off.

Another time, in the winter, a blizzard had drifted our road shut. Jim called his office to tell them he wouldn't be in, though he hated to miss that day when he was to brief an Air Force General. I called my supervisor to say I couldn't get in, and she asked when the road would be open, for she would send someone to get me.

In April, when Jim got a raise, I quit that job.

It gave me time to work on the book again. It had come back from Southern Publishing with a very nice letter, saying they had considered it for three months, but felt it wasn't something they could use right then. They suggested other publishers, but I sent it off, finally, to a different company.

The work on the book was a different concern than the worry over the boys' schooling. There was no satisfactory solution to their problems, though Jimmy was willing to work all summer as well as in the winter to help pay for his tuition. We thought Mark would be happy at the Academy too, and sent him there when he began ninth grade. He was about a year below level in all subjects except spelling, in which he was two years below level.

Mark disliked being away for home, and Paul announced that under no circumstance would he leave home to attend the Academy. We went to the Academy to visit Jimmy and Mark on the weekends. Their grades were average. Then in January, when Jim was in New York City on a business trip, I received a call from Jimmy who told me Mark and a friend had been playing around and his friend had hit Mark in the stomach. Mark was in severe pain and had been taken to the hospital and the doctor wanted to see Jim and me the next morning.

Jim was still in New York; I would have to go alone and fill out the papers. My fear of filling out papers was equal to my fear of not knowing what was wrong with Mark. Mary Shay was in Texas, so I called another friend, Jean, and asked her to go with me. She was moving into a new home that day, but she dropped everything to go with me.

She loved Mark dearly. She filled out the papers and stayed with me, while the urologist explained that Mark was born with horseshoe kidneys, and because the tubes were too small, he would have to have surgery on both kidneys. He told me Mark also had internal bleeding. Mark was in the hospital for two weeks, then came home to await surgery. He spent the month of July in the hospital, having surgery on one kidney, and the following January through mid-February was hospitalized for surgery on the other kidney.

Mark was attending Damascus High School when he was able to go to school. He was popular at school, had many friends, but had lost interest in classroom learning. He was good at sports, but because of the kidney problem, he had to give them up.

By 1976, the quality of education at the Academy had slipped, so in January 1976, we withdrew Jimmy from the Academy and enrolled him in Damascus High School, where Mark was going. Both boys graduated in the same year. Mark had accumulated enough credits to graduate at the end of 11th grade.

Our private school tuition expenses for Paul and John, in the Seventh Day Adventist School in Frederick had grown, and I felt once more that I should try to get a job. I agreed to take physical and psychological examinations to apply for a job through the Office of Rehabilitation in Montgomery County. I was frightened of the psychologist, as well as the psychological test. The first thing the psychologist did was to hand me a paper and pencil, with no explanation. My first thought was that I had to

WRITE. This upset me, so I asked him "Did you ever test a learning disability before?"

He replied, "I have not tested a learning disability before, but I have tested a person with a learning disability before."

I don't remember what I said to him, but he told me I was cynical. In my opinion, the test was silly. How you can tell a person's true IQ from that test, I'll never understand. My highest scores were in the verbal part of the tests. I did very well in this area. He read the tests to me, but this didn't mean that I had the background or understanding to know how to do the puzzles or draw diagrams. An individual with a learning disability who is tested with pencil and paper is tested in his areas of weakness, not his strengths.

The psychologist was in a hurry and asked me to take part of the tests home so my husband could read them to me. This was a test to help find out what kind of job I would like. As I was leaving his office, he asked me to tell him in ten words or less what I would like to do.

I answered, "Write."

He was writing something down, and slowly looked up at me, not saying a word.

With Jim reading the test to me, I knew I could make it say anything that I wanted, and I did. I wanted it to say I should be a writer, and it did. It also said I should be a librarian.

Since John and Paul were attending school in Frederick and I drove them daily, the rehabilitation counselor transferred my file to Frederick. She told me I could get a job in the Federal Government without testing if the Rehabilitation Office certified that I could do it. I felt hopeful, since Fort Detrick, a government installation, was located in Frederick. When I arrived at the Rehabilitation Office in Frederick, the counselor noticed Jim's salary and said to me, "With your husband's salary, you don't need to work."

I explained that due to my children being in private schools, we needed the money badly. He said they had a job for someone to take calls and write down names of callers. I told him I couldn't do that type of work because of my inability to spell names and addresses.

He said, "How about volunteer work?"

I wondered how that would help the money situation, but told him I was now tutoring first and second graders in reading. He said I would be hearing from him, but I never did.

Paul returned to the public school system when he started ninth grade. He meant what he said; he would not go to the Academy and live away from home.

Now it was time for John's re-entry. I went to the school to review his file, and saw a notation of a confidential file on our family. I asked about it and he dismissed my question saying I could go to the Area 5 office and review the files on my family.

I wrote a letter, with help, to our Superintendent of Schools, Dr. Charles M. Bernardo, asking him to look into the situation, and to locate all files on my family, and bring them to a central location for my review. Within days he answered and directed that all files be collected for my review – in five different schools.

My friend Mary Shay went with me and read these files to me, and she took notes.

By the time we found all such files, there were 15 of them. I did not find a file on myself. I had copies of the files made for myself, then had the original files destroyed (I hope). The concern and personal involvement of Dr. Bernardo was a welcome change from the attitudes and policies of the previous Superintendent.

To my surprise, a letter dated December 15, 1969, from the Supervisor of Special Education to Dr. Martin LaVor, who worked for Congress, was in the folders. Part of the letter said:

It appears the Howell boys (James, Paul, Mark, and John) have long been identified as children with reading problems, and they have had the advantage of special reading instruction for several years. All of the boys have had individual psychological and psychometric testing, and recommendations for placement and services have been determined through team analysis and consensus.

Although the children's home school is the White Grounds Road School in Boyds, Maryland, it was decided by Montgomery County special educators that attendance at the Poolesville Elementary School would allow them the opportunity for more frequent and more specialized attention. The boys are enrolled in regular classes and all four receive one hour of individualized special reading instruction each day from the school reading teacher, and one half hour of individual instruction from the special education teacher. This individual instruction is, of course, in addition to the regular instruction from their class teacher.

Mr. Celaschi (Supervisor of Appraisal and Placement) informed me the children are all of normal intelligence fine looking boys, friendly and blend in very well with the school population. He further added that "the children's teachers agree they are making progress and are, in terms of placement, in the best situation available with the county...."

Could it be, I wondered, that I misunderstood what happened at Poolesville in 1969? Then I wondered, September to December was four months of special help in reading, not several years. Who was teaching the Special Education class while the teacher was tutoring my boys for two hours a day? Who was teaching for the reading teachers' class two hours a day? There were no aides in the classrooms at that time. I thought the statement that the boys had had special reading instruction for several years was a broad interpretation of what had happened.

By now, almost all of my hopes of ever learning to read well were gone. I thought that God had left me. Now I could read all of John 15 and I felt John 15:7, "Anything you ask in my name, I will give to you," was not for me. Everybody else, but not me.

I never would be able to read or write well. It would always be very hard for me.

If I didn't have the boys and feel so frightened that they were going to face life as I did, I would have given up completely. But the hard fact was that, if my boys were not going to be in serious trouble with reading and spelling, God was all the hope I had. No matter how much other people tried to encourage me, I knew that they didn't understand how serious this problem was. So I couldn't leave my God because I knew that when it came right down to my problem, He was all I had. Although I was alone with Him so much and in such pain, I was still totally confused about His love.

When I tried to read the Bible, one of the verses that it kept opening to was: "Look, I place in Zion a stone that will make people stumble, a rock that will make them fall. But whoever believes in him will not be disappointed." (*Romans 9:33 GNT*)

I was not only very disappointed in my God, but I was also very afraid. Why did I care? I thought that other people's children are going to suffer from this problem and they don't even know it. Their children will live like others who had been illiterate. It's not new to our society. At least mine were getting some help, but most of these children wouldn't get any help at all. No help at all.

So mine were in good shape compared to most. Besides, Jimmy, Mark and Paul could long ago read and spell better than I can. Others tried to tell me my children would be okay. But when I tried to read or write and it was so hard to do even the simplest words, I knew I had to do all I could to help my children or I would not be able to live with myself.

I knew the only way I could be freed from the burden was to walk away from my God, to turn my back on Him and all He demanded. The day came when I was so tired and worn down I was going to do just that. I got up from my chair and walked to the window. I tried to face Him in my soul so I could break away. But as I tried to reject God, I found I couldn't, for I found that no matter where it took me, I had to go with Him.

Chapter 11
Tutoring

Even though we had a relaxing summer before John went into ninth grade, it didn't get John off to a very good start in public school. I knew that all the boys were tired of school and to try to teach them more words was like pouring water into a bucket that was already full. John was probably envying his two older brothers for being through with high school. This added to the problem of going from a small school where he had good friends, into a school with over a thousand students, none of whom he knew.

I stopped tutoring that year. I was uneasy about John, and couldn't put my attention to other children. One month after school started, John's counselor called to say that his teachers were concerned because he could not do the class work. They wanted to put him in special classes for students with learning problems. There would be no more than 20 students in each class with four team teachers working together to give each child individual help.

John entered the class in October, and his fellow students began to ridicule him. In a month's time, he had not made any friends at school and was a very unhappy boy. One teacher was able to keep the situation under control during class time, but the other teachers were so concerned that they called me in for a conference.

They felt the psychological damage John might suffer would be serious. What they wanted me to do about what went on in the classroom I didn't quite understand, since they didn't think the problem was caused by John.

I decided to see if time would heal the situation and if not, we would take him out of school. To me, a diploma was not worth psychological damage to anyone. Eventually, John's peers eased off.

John got a job at a local gas station, working evenings and Saturdays. By tenth grade, he was in regular classes and even though he hated school, he could deal with it. But his closest friends were those from the Seventh Day Adventist School, and he still stayed in contact with them.

I was feeling easier about John, was bored with housework, and my thoughts turned again to tutoring. One day while I was working in the kitchen, I heard a knock at the door. I opened it to a tall, thin woman with black hair and a pale, frightened face. She introduced herself as Mrs. Anderson, and told me that her daughter was dyslexic, and that she would like to talk to me about it. I asked her in.

Mrs. Anderson went on to say that her daughter had been tested psychologically at a local college. A friend had recommended me to her. I explained to her my own problem and told her I would be glad to help her daughter if I could, but I was only able to tutor up to a third grade level. Her daughter, Sue, was in fourth grade in a private school and was reading on a third grade level, according to the test.

I urged Mrs. Anderson to get help for her daughter immediately and recommended another tutor whom I had met through Jean. I knew how important it was to get started as early in the child's life as possible. I explained that even though I could take her daughter back to the beginning sounds and then move up from first grade level in tutoring, she would still have to be taught syllables, which I could not do. Though I could read many syllables, I wouldn't know the words separated from the context of the sentence.

Mrs. Anderson was so anxious about her daughter that I felt sorry for her. She left and called me later to tell me that the tutor I recommended had tested her daughter. She was indeed dyslexic and needed tutoring, but the tutor did not have time to do it. She was a reading teacher for a private school and her schedule after school was full. She recommended to Mrs. Anderson that I tutor Sue until she had enough space for her. She would check her progress once a month.

So, once more I was drawn back into tutoring. Later, the tutor had no openings and asked me to continue tutoring Sue. I was flattered that she felt I was able to teach her, because I knew she was a skillful tutor. I knew my weaknesses and didn't know how I could get Sue on grade level.

Mrs. Anderson and I agreed that she would work with Sue and me when we did syllables.

I will never understand the patience of this young girl. As we moved into the fourth grade level, when we came to a word that neither of us knew, we had to wait until her mother came to pick her up and ask her what the word was. Mrs. Anderson took it in stride and never showed any impatience. Due to Sue's hard work, she was on grade level in less than two years, by the time she entered sixth grade.

Often I wondered how I, with so many problems in reading and spelling, could be of any help to others. I believe partly that it was because I was honest with them about my problems. I had learned the skill of tutoring; it's just the words I didn't know. However, I truly believe it purely an act of God that I was so good at it.

That summer I found myself tutoring eight students, six days a week, to get them on grade level before the new school term began. This time they were all students in the public schools, and I realized only one or two of them would be up to grade level by the fall term.

I knew if I continued tutoring public school students, I would have to go to the schools for conferences, but for some reason, I was looking forward to it. This time, I would not be so emotionally involved as I had been with my own children.

At first, after the school year started, I was amused with the comments from the teachers and administrators who told parents basically the same things they had told me so many years ago, using the same educational jargon and with the same vagueness.

The parents whose child I was tutoring felt more comfortable with me at the meetings, but the staff seemed to ignore anything I had to say. It didn't take the parents long to realize this, and it made them angrier than they already were.

When I started tutoring one girl, the school staff, with the mother present, told me they didn't care how I taught her; she was a sweet girl and they loved her, but they were at the end of their rope. At the end of 3 months of tutoring, a new classroom teacher, hostile to me, bragged about how well the girl was doing because of the structured classroom. The other two teachers, who had been at the previous meeting, had no comment. I left the meeting early and the mother called to tell me the classroom teacher had said she should be sure she was getting her money's worth for this tutoring, which she thought was making the child too dependent on me.

"Mrs. Howell," the mother said, "I felt very bad and didn't know what to say to her." The woman didn't tell the teacher that I charged her nothing for tutoring, even though some parents were now paying me $15.00 an hour. She went on to let me know that she knew how much my tutoring had done for her daughter, and that she was very sorry for the teacher's comments.

"Forget it," I told her. I went on to explain that school people seem to be threatened by outsiders and I was used to being treated like that by the educators.

The need for tutors was increasing, and I couldn't see where they were going to come from. Every time I talked to a parent who was upset, and often crying, I felt the pressure to help. When parents came to me for help, they had usually tried everything else. The school had told them their child was learning with special help from the reading specialist or the reading teacher, but when the parents did not see their child reading, as he should, they often blamed the child for not trying. I didn't like to think of what that did to the child. Parents often felt guilty, asking, "What did I do to my child?"

After I told parents about my own learning problems, I assured them they hadn't done anything to their child to cause the learning problems. It is important for parents to understand that a learning problem is not the end of the world, and with the proper tutoring/teaching, they will learn the skills that are necessary for learning to read. It is hard to convince parents that, though the problem is serious, it can be corrected if it is begun early enough. When the reading skills improve, the class work will also usually improve.

Parents have a hard time accepting learning disabilities in their children. They tell me their children's behavior problems are no worse than any other child. They say it is a matter of not liking to do their homework or forgetting to bring the assignment home, or that their child is lazy and does not like school.

Some, when they hear the word "dyslexic" or "learning disability" immediately think of brain damage. My heart almost breaks for them so I try to tell them that languages are symbols and grunts made by man for communication. English is one of the hardest languages in the world to learn, as it is a collection from all over the world. It is not consistent.

When a singer cannot dance, we do not call it brain damage or emotional problems. Or, I tell them, if a runner can't ice skate, we don't say he has a low IQ. If someone is not an artist, we don't think of him as having something wrong with him. We just say he is not artistic. Or when an accomplished musician can't sing, we don't think there is a problem. So why, I ask parents, should we think someone who has a hard time learning to read is brain damaged, emotionally disturbed, has a low IQ, or is just plain lazy?

The fact that so many Americans are sloppy about the way they speak and write this difficult language makes it even harder for those with learning disabilities in language. When I test a student, I sit across from her so I can see her face as she tries to read. I can see right away the problem by the pattern of the words she doesn't know, and how much guessing she is doing. Some students read too fast. Then their eyes pick up beginning letters or a part of a word, and they mix up words that look alike, such as "then" and "there." They may know the words when I call them to their attention, but read so fast, they don't realize they are getting them wrong.

I tell them to relax, that I am not going to do brain surgery on them. When I check for spelling, I dictate sentences. Here again, I can often tell right away how bad the problem is by the pattern of misspelled words. For instance, I dictate "like" and they write "lake," I dictate "soon" and they write "soone." Even the way they hold the pencil, rigidly, is an indication of improper instruction.

One time when Jean was tutoring me, she gave me a reading comprehension test. I was to read a short page silently, and then she would ask me questions about it. She knew I could read almost all the words. The story was about a farmer and two geese. One of the geese died. The farmer took gasoline in a can and poured it over the goose to burn it. I saw the word "gas" and mixed "can" with "car." When Jean questioned me about what I had read, I told her a completely different story from the one that was on the page.

The older the child is, the less he likes being slowed down. I can remember how frustrated I became when Jean would slow me down, and I try to be very patient with the children I tutor. I use a pencil to go along the lines on the top of the sentences, while a student holds a marker under the sentence, and I tap the word if they misread it. I would hold them back firmly, saying, "Slow down." It was more than a couple of my students could bear.

One boy hit the pencil and knocked it across the room. Of course, I didn't take that too well. I let him know I would keep slowing him down, and he would keep being frustrated, but he had to learn to see the words accurately. This kind of thing is made worse in a classroom setting, because everything is based on a period of time and the teacher is always encouraging them to hurry. For children with this kind of problem, it is the worst thing a teacher can do.

Classroom teachers, who push too fast, combined with the child's own frustration of not being able to learn, makes it hard to slow them down. It is like driving 90 miles an hour and being thrown into reverse. Often, it was more a matter of teaching the child to discipline his mind. If he could decode the words, but had poor comprehension, it was usually because his thinking was too fast.

Many times, stopping this is almost as difficult as teaching words. These children need a great deal of repetition, and subject matter, which is short and straight to the point.

The child who has difficulty hearing short vowel sounds must be taught these basic sounds. Most children don't have as much difficulty hearing the long vowel sounds. When I tried tutoring in small groups, I found it impossible. One child in the group had more difficulty hearing sounds than others did, so they would fall behind quickly.

When parents ask how I can teach these children when the schools cannot, I point out the need for trained tutors on a one-to-one basis. The school system, with its reading specialists, should be able to help a lot of these children, but children as handicapped as I am need long-term tutoring, usually from the first to the fourth grades. The later the problem is discovered and diagnosed, the longer the tutoring must continue.

Some students, whom the schools haven't been able to reach, are very capable. For example, I started to tutor a boy when he was in the second grade. He was reading on a first grade level. After tutoring for about six months, he was reading on an eighth grade level without too much teaching from me. I believe he would have outgrown most of his problem, but the tutoring saved him a lot of learning time and frustration. I told his mother that he was gifted. She didn't think he was, but when he was in the fifth grade, he was placed in the gifted program.

Parents have told me that after their children have been in tutoring for a short time, they become more self-confident, easier to satisfy, and a pleasure to have around. When these children learn that the problem is not their fault and that there are many others like them, a great burden is lifted from them. One parent told me, when she came in for tutoring one day, that her son, who had never read before tutoring began, would now sit on the commode, reading or singing, and read at night before he went to sleep.

Another parent said to me in a concerned voice, that her daughter was talking to herself in the mirror. I laughed and explained, "I taught her to do that, to watch her mouth as she repeated the words and sounds."

When I first asked at the elementary school to train parents to be tutors, I told them that it had taken me most of my lifetime to learn to read, and then to tutor. I said I couldn't train, in a short period of time, parents who have no real concept of this problem and who might become too impatient and emotionally involved with the students. A tutor, or teacher, who does not have a feeling for, or understanding of the problem can do more harm than good to a child, and end up blaming the child instead of their own lack of skill. Yet in the end I trained three tutors. There is no excuse that I accept for not teaching a child to read. I don't expect a bunch of Eric Hoffers or straight-A students, so I don't allow excuses like "low IQ," "emotional problems," or "home environment" as reasons for a child's not learning.

One of the tutors, Trish Carey, was working on a Master's Degree in Special Education. She likes to argue with me about these problems. She is more interested in learning disabilities across the board than I am. I specialize in those who can't handle the basic skills. This isn't to say I'm not sympathetic with the others who are having problems, but those in the gifted group who can read and spell and do basic math very well should not have so much time spent on them when there are children who are illiterate and will graduate as such.

I tell Trish, a psychological test is not worth three hurrahs in hell when it comes to problems in basic skills. All such testing does is show there is a problem, which we already know. The depth of the problem doesn't show until tutoring begins. Trish is a spunky gal with a great sense of humor and a heart as big as the world. She wants so badly for each child, no matter what the problem, not to suffer in the classroom.

I don't trust the IQ which shows on psychological testing because of the test I had taken, and I have seen too many students whose school records show a low IQ when all they had was a severe learning disability. As the learning disability is dealt with in proper tutoring, the IQ goes up. Trish knows more about the psychological testing than I do and, when I need to read a psychological for a student, I call her. The only reason I try to read them is to make parents feel better.

After I had done what I could to train the tutors, and we saw the need for tutors was so great, we decided we would get a grant from the government and continue to tutor children free of charge. The children who needed help the most came from poor homes where parents couldn't afford to pay anything. One mother who joined us was going to do all the paper work. She got tax papers to file for a tax exemption, and papers to file for a grant.

When I saw those papers, I couldn't believe it. It made me think of removing a splinter from your finger with a double-barreled shotgun. We worked on the papers for a time, then felt completely hopeless about getting them done, and gave up.

I realized then that recognition of the value of tutors was going to take many more years. Once more we were tied up with the bureaucracy of the system and again I found myself working alone because the others whom I had trained couldn't afford to do it free.

Chapter 12
The Last of School?

Though I had learned, through many struggles, how to help other people's children, I could neither tutor John nor convince him to be tutored. He had so much frustration in the school that the classroom setting turned him off. He didn't want to make any effort to learn, and I couldn't blame him.

John was in the 11th grade, with enough credits to graduate if he passed his courses that year. I hated to see him suffer through any more school, and felt he, as well as his brothers, would have been better off at a good trade school, if there had been one. John's counselor was working with John to help him graduate at the end of 11th grade. Five days before graduation, the counselor called to say John had not passed the history test and could not graduate because he needed ½ credit.

John was crushed, Jim was furious, and I went up against the administrators again, but it did no good. I went through all the channels I could think of, but it was only because John went to summer school that he got the half credit he needed to complete high school. He had been going to school for 13 years. He was more than ready to be out of it. His diploma was given to him at the end of those three weeks of summer school.

Now all my boys were out of school. I would have no more battles with the system. Once more, I too, was free of school. Yet I couldn't stay away. By fall I was ready to tackle the problem again. Someone had to help those children who would soon be over their heads in words, symbols, and sounds, which made no sense to them.

I went to our neighborhood school as a volunteer tutor, for I had found tutoring at home to be lonely and depressing. It was hard for me to work with the parents who were so upset over their children, as well as the children themselves who were so frightened and confused. I appreciated the support I got at the school. Though I was treated graciously, and the relationship between the teachers and me was cordial, I soon learned that there was far more talk about learning disabilities than there was help.

I worked five days a week, seven hours a day, on tutoring, with occasional breaks. Every now and then I would get this book out and work on it. So far, three publishers had kept it, considered it, and returned it.

Since the only books I had ever read were books written on the third grade level, I wasn't sure what I should do with it. I wanted it short because I hoped the readers would be those who have had the same problems I did, although, illiterates would not be able to read this or any other book. I wondered if 64 typewritten pages was too short, but I figured if Thomas Payne could start the Revolutionary War with a book of 40 pages, surely I could describe the effects of a learning disability in 64 pages.

I asked Mary, who was going to college, if she would find someone to help me. Right away she did. He was an English teacher at the school. He was very excited about doing the book and, like many others, he said it was well written. But for some reason he told me that I was not a writer and would never be.

I think he thought that someone else had written it. I said nothing about his feelings and waited to see what he would do with it. Although he talked about the book a lot, after a year he had done nothing and I learned that he did not have a Ph.D. and had never published a book, as he had told me. Since I was uneasy about him, I decided not to continue with him.

Tutoring became more and more frustrating, not because of the students, but because so little was known about learning problems. I still had many concerns about Special Education.

One mother came to me because of her concerns about the possibility of her son being placed in Special Education. She had dropped out of school in the tenth grade, after going through Special Education classes during her school years, saying she "never learned a thing." She didn't want her son, Robert, to go through the same thing.

I began to work with both Mrs. Poole and Robert. Mrs. Poole had spent her life up to that point believing she was retarded. The damage this has done to her may never be corrected, but she hopes her children won't have to go through their lives with the same bad feelings about themselves.

With tutoring, Robert was able to learn to read at grade level, and do math problems his mother was also learning to do. Yet he was still unable to keep up with his class, and was put into Special Education class because the school itself offers no tutoring programs. I protested strongly and clearly, which only seemed to make the teachers more determined to put him in Special Education. I stopped tutoring at this point because the child was caught in the middle of my methods and the teachers' lack of support. I recognized his two younger sisters to have learning disabilities, which the teachers also realized, but not in time to begin the help early in the school year.

I consider myself, Mrs. Poole, and her children, as three generations of people with learning problems.

Dyslexia is a big word now, yet educators still know very little about learning problems.

John graduated from Asbury College. All four of our boys are now married and have children. All of them are working hard and enjoying life.

I was beginning to think that it was really not God's will that this book be finished. But like the past, when things seemed hopeless, someone was waiting to guide me through. Ginger Gibson, a writer and editor, was my saving grace. We worked long and hard to finish the book.

I still long to read *COMMON SENSE* and many other books, but find it impossible. I can, however, read a revised edition of the Bible, although I can read for only a short time, as my mind will tire quickly. I still don't write letters, checks, etc., as not knowing how to spell well enough is too frustrating. However, when it comes to writing this book or stories and poems, I endure the frustration and drive everybody around me crazy asking them how to spell words. I can handle this kind of frustration because after finishing a poem or story, I have such feeling of satisfaction and accomplishment that I have never known in my life.

It makes me wonder sometimes about this long, painful road that I have traveled and whether or not I am finished with schools. Why, I ask myself, did God insist that I walk this road, only giving me freedom of it long enough to take a breath, then on with it again?

How long will it take before people realize the importance of proper teaching of reading and spelling? Fourteen years ago when I first learned why I lived in fear, loneliness and darkness, there was almost no talk about this problem. Now, even though the cry for help, and the money to support it has increased, illiteracy itself is also increasing. I can't help but wonder if I will have to tutor and fight with the school systems to be sure that my grandchildren will not be illiterate. However, I have learned one thing for sure in this struggle:

When we do our best with what we are given, God will take it from there and work all things together for good.

Let me try to reson with you to sent a child to school for 12 years to go into socidy not ablem to suiv because they cannot read or spell is unfair and very crul and you have not right to expce anything in reture from them but full bloom anger. The seed was planed tha frist year of thare school.

Chapter 13
Retired to Antique Dealing

It was January the first in 1989 when Jim retired. We spent the next year relaxing and traveling. I was getting bored, with running around and doing nothing, as I called it. So, I thought I would like to go into the antique business. We had been collectors for years. Jim was very reluctant but he gave in and let me try. It was my plan to be in the antique business about three years then find something else to do. Jim was 55 years old and I was 52; it was too early to completely retire.

I had not been tutoring for about three years and I was glad to be away from tutoring. Tutoring was very hard for me; when I did tutor, I not only had a hard time with words, but faced the two things that had defeated me all my life: *reading* and *writing*.

My boys were all married by now and we had six grandchildren. I often wondered what kind of schooling they were going to have. I had learned more than ever not to trust what educators say. I had also learned not to trust their so-called "good grades." By now I was very tired and simply did not have the strength to warn the boys that they could not trust what all teachers say about their own children's reading and writing abilities. I knew from bitter experience, if problems weren't discovered by the fourth grade it was too late to correct the problem completely.

The higher grade level a child goes in school, the more information a child is required to handle. This means that the speed and accuracy with which a child reads and writes is very important. In years past people could get away with being poor readers and spellers. They worked in blue-collar jobs where reading and spelling were not as important. Today, with college as the goal and the amount of information that must be dealt with in this computer technology age, it is very different.

I thought about all of these things, and I also thought that my boys had lived through all of this; they should have learned, from their own experience, to take reading and writing very seriously. So, I stayed out of their business as much as I could, and turned all my attention to the antique business.

We opened two booths in two separate antique malls in Frederick, MD. After a year, I could see that there was a better way to sell our merchandise. We had opened a show case in the Antique Station and sales were better there than the other two places combined. So I decided to close the two places and open a booth in the Antique Station and Jim agreed.

Some of the dealers at the station worked in their booths on weekends so I decided to do the same. Jim played golf on Saturdays and I worked at our booth. On Sundays we both worked together. Being there increased our sales. We could talk to customers, answer their questions, and negotiate on prices;

bargaining in the antique business is a must. Jim and I increased our hours until it eventually turned into a full time job. We started with one booth – now we have nine.

Jan Lanahan, the manager, took great interest in how the dealers businesses were doing. She was professional and supportive, which made her easy to work with. She also had a great sense of humor.

I still had a hard time with names and mixed up sounds which sounded alike to me. I often called Jan "Jan Learnahan." One of the dealers corrected me in front of Jan and Jan immediately commented, "My name is Jan Lend-a-hand." I also called her "Jan Dear," and she called me "Dory Dear." Names are so difficult for me that I referred to people who I didn't know as "Ma'am" and "Sir." However, I must admit that I often forget the names of even the people I know.

Rita Ward was hired as an employee shortly after we opened our first booth. She, too, was a loving person with a great sense of humor. I wanted to remember her name so I made a real effort. No matter how hard I tried to remember Rita's name, I couldn't. When I needed to use her name, I usually came up with a blank, or I would call her "Reba." I had known a "Reba" in the past.

Rita took it with good humor. I ended up calling her "Rebar" thereafter. We all had fun with my weakness for names and even had the employees and dealers calling each other by the wrong names on purpose. Names were not my only problem. I found that I had lost much of the spelling that I had learned through tutoring, simply because I was not using it.

Now I had another problem. Jim did all of the paper work and priced our merchandise. All items were paid for at the front desk. If the asking price was changed and Jim was not there, I had to write the name of the item and the agreed on price. I had no choice but to tell Jan about my spelling problem. Thereafter, Jan checked to make sure my spelling was correct, since the information was for their records. Much of the time, I got it right, because I copied the information off Jim's tags. Jan also checked my math; it was rare that mistakes were made. If Jim was not working, Rita, who by now was the assistant manager, took care of things.

Jan and Rita never let me know that they were "checking my spelling" but I could see them doing it from time to time. The staff was never unkind to me because of my problem with reading and writing. Never once was I ridiculed or made to feel uncomfortable. I have never been treated with so much respect as I was by the staff.

However, this was not true of a small group of dealers. There were over one hundred separate dealers at the antique station. Many were kind and considerate but one group seemed to think Jim and I were too successful. They talked behind our backs. My being illiterate seemed to make them feel that it was perfectly okay to say anything about me. It wasn't Jim that they went after with untruths. They accused me indirectly of being dumb, lazy, and a cheat. I would never lie, and can't understand people who do.

Before the Antique Station was an antique mall it had been a skating rink. It is a large, open building and every word that is spoken can often be heard. I knew some of these dealers were listening to every word being said in our booth, so I decided to give them something to hear. I hated to see them listening so much and not finding something to gossip about so I would make up stories and wait for the things I said to get back to me. They did.

We had a desk in our booth that Jim used to do our paper work. Above the desk we would post phone numbers and reminders. Some dealers would read our notes when we were not there. I caught them doing this several times when I entered the booth quietly. One time I walked up on an outside dealer looking at the notes, taking him by surprise. I said sarcastically, "May I help you?"

He jerked his head upward toward the picture hanging over the desk and said, "I'm just looking" and walked away quickly.

I thought I would give them something interesting to read. I took a piece of paper and wrote, "Call the White House every Saturday for furniture, 9-5. Ask for Sue." I showed the note to Jan so the FBI wouldn't get me and told her what I was doing and why. She laughed and said, "I love it, Dory."

Our furniture was intentionally scratched. Prisms were stolen from our lamps and chandeliers. Items were removed from our booth and placed in other booths. I felt these things would have happened more frequently if Jim and I were not there most of the time or Jan was not "on guard" to catch them. Jan was very aware of any activities going on in the building and was good at catching such things. She and I tried very hard but did not catch all the activities when they went on in our booth.

Jim and I had been in a bad car accident returning from a buying trip. Jim was hurt worse than I was and was in a great deal of pain. I was very worried about him, so I kept as much as I could from him. He didn't need these kinds of things to add to his problem.

Eventually this small group of disagreeable dealers moved out of the Antique Station and being at the Station is now very pleasant. The dealers include those with different philosophies and religions, which provide interesting and lively discussions. All the dealers are cordial, thoughtful and honest people.

I was learning something new every day in the antique business: the difference between "Antiques" and "Collectibles", how to identify them and the differences between a reproduction and a genuine antique. The nice dealers never hesitated to share their information with us but some other dealers would tell me to look it up, meaning to do my own research.

I was used to being alone and having to do my own research, so this situation was not new to me. Jim was very good at research but his interests in antiques and collectibles were in different areas than mine. Jim had learned by now not to give me too much advice, so he did his thing and I did mine. However, if I asked him to read to me, he would gladly do it.

Bob was another dealer who I enjoyed talking with. He was a very interesting man and knew the antique business well. I learned a lot from him. One day I was in his booth and he asked me to leave. I thought nothing of it as he was very busy. Our visits continued over time.

On one occasion he said to me, "Dory, I hope I have never hurt you." I knew he was referring to the day he asked me to leave.

I said, "Bob, you never hurt me. I thought you were just busy and that I was in your way."

He came in about once a month to restock his booth. He would often apologize for that incident and I would insist that he did not hurt my feelings. One day we were sitting on the front portico of the Station. We had taken a break to enjoy a few minutes of warmth outside. Bob had a lot of personal and health problems and he looked bad. He said to me, once more, "Dory, I hope I never hurt you, but one of the dealers has told me such awful things about you, and I believed him."

I named all the dealers I knew who had said terrible things about me. "They don't hurt me," I said to Bob, "but if you had said these things about me, it would hurt. But those dealers have to have someone to attack. If it wasn't me, they would attack each other."

Bob patted his heart and asked, "But doesn't it hurt in here?"

"Not from them," I told him.

"I have something to tell you," Bob said. I looked at him and waited to see what horror he was going to tell me that one of the dealers had said about me. "I'm gay," he said.

I smiled. "I have known that for years," I told him. He laughed; we talked some more then went back to work.

The next week I saw him from a distance and waved. The following week when we went in to work Jan said, "Dory, I want to talk to you. Let's walk." This is what we often did when we wanted to talk. She told me that Bob had been found dead in his home the day before. We were heart broken and I miss him to this day.

I had cleaned and repaired old things since I was twenty years old to use in my own house. Now I was doing it a lot in our own business. Stripping furniture to refinish, cleaning silver and gluing things often require using very strong chemicals. I enjoyed seeing old things restored to their original beauty and thought nothing of the chemicals I was using.

When my health began to deteriorate, I went to five different doctors. They found a large polyp in my gall bladder, and low blood sugar, but nothing else. I kept candy on hand for the sudden drops in blood sugar.

On two separate nights I woke with my body shaking so much it shook the bed. Other nights I had a hard time sleeping at all. One night I prayed, "God, if you don't send me help, I am not going to make it."

About a week later a dealer who had left the Station came to visit. She looked wonderful. She had lost weight and her skin looked great. I said to her, "Tina, you look great. What diet are you on?"

"I'm not on a diet," she told me. "I take herbs."

As soon as she said that, I knew that I would try herbs. She got me started with a procedure called "colon cleanse" and I ended up at the Common Market in Frederick. The herbalist who worked there answered all of my questions and showed me what books to buy that would explain the use of herbs. (Jim was not too impressed by herbs. He called the colon cleanse procedure a wallet cleanse.)

This all meant that I would have to read, once more, to learn all about herbs. Within a month I began to feel the healthful effects of using herbs.

Within three months, one of the dealers told me that she could see 100% improvement in my health. In this period of time I had learned that I was suffering from toxic poisoning and was a very sick woman. How much damage was done to my body I don't know as I am still struggling with the effects of toxic poisoning, even after five years. My symptoms were hypoglycemia, poor memory, exhaustion, kidney, lung problems, and gall bladder polyps.

I loved learning about herbs and experimenting with them. The books had short paragraphs describing the use of each herb. If I could not read a certain word, Jim would read it for me. If there was something that I needed to know about any certain herb that was over one page long, Jim would read it to me.

I am amused that we kill off certain herbs that we should be eating by spraying them with weed killers. I never use an herb without researching it. I suggest that anyone wanting to use herbs do the same thing, if they can read well enough to do this. After all, this is what this book is all about – *the ability to read.*

Chapter 14
The Importance of This Book

By now Jim was taking herbs at my insistence and his general health was improving, although he still had pain from the injuries received in our auto accident.

I still get upset by things that I cannot read and very frustrated when I come to words that I do not know. I still have a lot of rage in me and have a hard time controlling it. I often think that if I had been taught one word a day, how to spell it and how to read it, that would have taught me about 2,340 words in the thirteen years that I spent in school. I knew about 130 words when I graduated from high school, and could not spell most of them.

I get impatient with Jim when he takes too long to explain something that I ask him. Often I already know about the subject in question and ask for a small detail. When he goes on with a long explanation of the subject I yell, "Answer my question." When he does, I settle down.

When I hear professionals talking about the brain that people like me have, I think "So what if my brain is in my head upside down?" I feel I could have learned those 2,340 words in the thirteen years that I was in school if someone had tried to work with me. If I had learned to read and write I would not have needed educators' words of wisdom. I would have gladly learned the facts about any subject and learned the rest on my own, as I did anyway.

When I discovered that I had toxic poisoning I stopped using chemicals to clean antiques and collectibles. Mike R. and his employees would refinish and restore our furniture and did an excellent job of it. They took an interest in our business doing well and took pride in their work.

Our son Mark had gone into our business as a silent partner. Our son Paul's oldest daughter, Sandee, occasionally worked with us to earn some spending money when she was twelve years old. We enjoyed having her and the dealers enjoyed her company also. She could sell almost anything.

We now have eight grandchildren and I am still reluctant to get involved in their educational problems unless I am asked. Even then, I don't want to get involved. I have learned that things have not changed all that much in the school system.

To compound the learning problem, discipline has become a more serious problem. The shootings in schools are only one of the problems schools face. Teaching children how to read may be one of the last problems they deal with. I pray to my God, "Don't let one of my grandchildren be illiterate." I don't expect them to be like the philosopher Eric Hofer. I just ask that they not be illiterate, barely reading and spelling on a first grade level.

I do believe that my learning problems were compounded not only by poor teaching, but by malnutrition when I was a child. Our boys never had a nutrition problem according to the standards of this society. However, the lack of good nutrition is not dependent on the amount of food available but the choice of healthy or non-healthy foods. I am sure too much sugar and fatty food interferes with the learning process.

Upon graduation from high school, all four of our boys could read and write well enough to be successful in their chosen fields.

Last year Jan Lanahan developed a health problem and had to retire. It broke my heart. Jim said that I cried all day. He didn't know, but I cried all night also. It was strange because I never had any contact with Jan outside of the Antique Station. She never once sat down in my booth just to chat; she was always very professional and never fraternized with the dealers.

Courtney, our granddaughter, did work with us in our business some week-ends to earn extra money just as our granddaughter, Sandee, used to do. Courtney cannot come to work unless her school home work is up to date. All school children seem to have a lot of home work these days.

Courtney gets good grades and works long hours, after school, on her homework. She enjoys working with us and is disappointed when she isn't able to come. I think the school system should extend the school day so students could get their homework done at school and be free of school work until the next day. Even adults don't like to take work home with them, and children get tired, too.

One Saturday when we were working at our business, a new dealer in the station, Judy R., came in and sat down to talk. I asked her if she had another job, as most dealers do. She said, "I am a literary agent and I am looking for manuscripts. Do you know anyone who has written a manuscript?"

I was in total shock. She knew nothing about me and had no idea I had written anything. She looked at me, and must have seen something in my face.

"Do you have a manuscript that you have written, Dory?" she asked me.

I said, "Yes."

"I would like to see it," she told me.

"I will think about it," I answered. I thought about it for almost three weeks and remained very reluctant to let her see it, because I knew nothing about her and am always on guard in dealing with people I don't know. Then I thought, "Maybe this is God's will, since it just came out of the blue." Maybe when she sees my manuscript she might think it was not good enough to be published. Then I wouldn't have to worry about it." It had been in a dresser drawer in my bedroom for the past fifteen years. I thought, "Why not let her see it?"

I took it to her. She read it and said she liked it and would like to try to get it published. I told her that I would think about it. Over the next several months, Judy and I talked about the manuscript. I also talked to Jim about having the manuscript published. At first he was reluctant because he thought this was "all in the past." Finally he said, "What have you got to lose?"

Even then it took me a long time to say yes. I know it was difficult for Judy to deal with me, but she was a nice person, and patient. Jim read three different publishers' contracts to me, and I rejected all three. Finally Jim said, "I wish you would sign one." The fourth contract came and, after some changes, I did sign it.

"Here I go again," I thought. This meant that I would have to update the manuscript. I thought I had thrown away all of my background files which would support my manuscript, but there they were in another dresser drawer. This meant struggling with reading and writing once more as well as reading the manuscript again.

It was very painful to remember the past. I had changed the title from I CLIMBED A MOUNTAIN to STAND STRAIGHT AND GROW TALL. Years ago I had a dream that I was standing among huge redwood trees, so tall I could not see the top of them. A voice said, "Name your book STRAIGHT AND TALL. I added "Stand" and "Grow."

Jim said that he would work with me and help me any time that I asked him. He would take dictation. The problem was that we had different writing styles and I was impatient with this. For example, Jim would write, "The teacher put me in a stressful situation," and I would write, "The teacher scared me to death." Needless to say, we had a hard time.

However, we got through it, thanks to Ginger Gibson's editing skills. I had called Ginger and told her that my manuscript was going to be published and that I had to update it with two chapters. I asked her if I could pay her to edit the two chapters. She knew me and my writing and I trusted her completely. She was surprised to hear from me and happy to hear that the manuscript was going to be published. I asked her to think about helping me and to give me a call when she made her decision.

The next morning she called me and said that she would be glad to edit the last two chapters and help me as much as she could. She said that she would not charge me anything to help me because she was not a professional editor.

I said to her, "Ginger, I don't know about being a professional editor, but I do know that several people who have read my manuscript have told me they couldn't put it down until they had finished it." I also told Ginger, "I lived this and did my best to write about it, as you well know, but if nobody can read it, it does little good. My cause, teaching reading and writing, is far more important than I am. I would gladly pay you for your help." Ginger said no, she would not charge anything for her help.

When I had to read the manuscript again, after fifteen years, the one thing that came to my mind was the kind of people who gladly helped me when I needed help. Looking back I could see that God had not left me. He was right with me all the time. Life was never meant to be easy. I learned that very early. God did not promise that it would be easy. As a matter of fact, Jesus said, "Pick up your cross and follow me." Sometimes that cross can be very heavy.

Now I am eighty-one years old. I sometimes wonder what has happened to my students. One of them, George Ullrich is now a psychiatrist.

I was thirty two years old when I announced to anyone who would listen that I was illiterate. I thought there was nothing bad left that anyone could do to me that they had not already done as far as learning is concerned. I was wrong about that. There is something about the word "illiterate" that can bring out pre-conceived ideas that people have.

Now, being eighty-one years old, I have dealt with all kinds of people from the most liberal to the most conservative thinkers, from the most tolerant to the most intolerant. Those who would never think of themselves as being unfair can be very cruel, thinking they have the right to be cruel when dealing with someone who is illiterate. They talked down to me and lied about me without a moment's hesitation.

Their treatment reminds me of baby chickens when they hatch. The strongest chicks will peck the weakest chick to death. Don't misunderstand me. A few well chosen, direct words will get most of their attention. I am not talking about being unkind or rude but using well chosen, direct words. When they learn that I am not what they thought I was, I frighten them. Several people have told me this. When I was dealing with the public school system, one of my friends said to me, "I never want you mad at me."

I answered, "I judge people by their intent, and you would never make me mad at you."

Before you, the reader, think of these people as not being very nice, what is your own opinion of someone who is illiterate? - A person who is also a born-again Christian and from West Virginia? I am considered by other dealers to be a skillful business person now, and my decision to finish this book was very difficult. Jim and I decided that for the sake of our grandchildren, and others, I should do it.

My parents paid taxes and sent me to public schools. I was willing to learn. The teaching failed me. I did not fail alone.

Three Selections
from the
Poetry and Prose of
Dolores Howell

Unteachable

When I was a child in school
It was said to my parents who valued education
"Your child is unteachable."

"Unteachable" it was said
By those who are teachable,
By those in the know.

Those in the know marked my records "unteachable."
Many believed "Unteachable" was me.
I was in a school for those who were teachable.

I was ignored and ridiculed
Because "unteachable" was me.
I didn't learn much – I was "unteachable."

One day I memorized a poem
A poem for the teachable, and me.
A poem to improve my thinking and myself.

A poem which said what I should be
Even though I was "unteachable."
I took it with me through the years.

Even though I couldn't read and write
Because I was "unteachable."
I have carried the poem in my mind all these years.

I wrote a poem of my own years later,
Even though I couldn't read and write.
It was a good poem, I was told by someone "teachable."

So I wrote another, and another good poem
Good enough to be published,
Said those who are teachable.

"But wait," I said, "that can't be."
"Only the teachable can write poetry
Good enough to be published."

My poem cannot be
Because we all can see I am "unteachable."
Poetry is not for me, only the teachable can write poetry.

Dolores Howell

My Tutor

The day before yesterday
My tutor taught me to hope
Just a spark of hope
I held tightly to this spark
And yesterday my tutor taught me to spell hope.

Today, I never dreamed how big that spark would grow.
I know all the knowledge I have is small,
So small, that what is important today
May not be important tomorrow.

But there is one lesson I have learned from my tutor:
"Just one," the hope I was taught the day before yesterday
Did not change yesterday, or today.
I know it will not change in the darkness of tomorrow.

With that hope, my tutor opened a door for me;
I entered a room that I thought was the biggest room in
the world
I passed through that room to find that it was
But the entrance hall.

Dolores Howell

Life of an Apple

A story by Dolores Howell

Not long ago, in a big orchard outside of town, there stood a small apple tree. It had apples for the first time. On this tree was a very small apple. Someday he would grow up to be a big apple, and be picked by someone for something great, like apple juice or something else real big. He could hardly wait; someday he would be proud.

One day the apple was sunning himself. He was growing bigger and beginning to blush a little. He was very happy. That night he began to feel a little pain in his core. He thought, "What is this! A good apple has no pain!" The pain began to grow. "Oh my!" he said. "What will I do?" He thought and thought. What could it be?

There was a pear tree near the apple tree. The apple didn't want the other apples to know that he had a pain in his core, so he couldn't ask them about his problem. "I'll ask the pear next to me," he thought.

"Mr. Pear," the apple said, "can you help me? I have a pain in my core. Can you tell me what it is?"

The pear was shocked to be asked to help an apple. "A pain in your core?" asked the pear. "Oh, my!" The pear said. "You must have a worm in your core."

"A *worm*," the apple said. "Not a *worm*! No one will want me now! What will I do?" He cried and cried. "Who…will…want…me…now?"

Weeks passed, and workers came to pick the apples. One of the men picked the "not so small anymore" apple and noticed it had a worm hole and tossed it on the ground. Now the apple was really hurting very badly after hitting the ground. He just lay there, so hurt that he wasn't good for anything.

His blush began to turn brown. He felt very soft. He was tired, and it was night time. He thought, "My life is for nothing." And he went to sleep for good.

Spring came very early the next year. The apple and pear tree flowered. The sun was very warm and everything was green. Near the apple tree there was a brown spot that was once an apple; in the middle of the spot was a little sprout. A seed had begun to grow from the sad apple.

One day there stood a big apple tree that once was the little apple. A man was picking apples from the tree. As he climbed down from the tree, he said, "There is not one worm in any of these apples."

Then the whole tree smiled. You couldn't see it smile, but it smiled.

155

A Note from the Editor - I did a search on-line with this entry:
    "famous Dyslexic people"
Below is one of many lists I found: *List of Dyslexic Achievers*
from www.dyslexia.com. This site has much more information
about these people as well as about Dyslexia. I encourage readers
to visit this site to read about these famous, Dyslexic people and
their many accomplishments.

Athletes:

Individual Sports:
    Bob May, Diamond Dallas Page, Greg Louganis, Jackie Stewart,
    Meryl Davis, Mohammad Ali

Team Sports:
    Caitlin Jenner, Duncan Goodhew, Magic Johnson, Nolan Ryan,
    Rex Ryan, Steve Redgrave

Business Leaders:
    Charles Schwab, Craig McCaw, David Neeleman, Gary Cohn,
    Henry Ford, Ingvar Kamprad, John T Chambers, Josh Almeida,
    Kevin O'Leary, O.D. McKee, Paul J. Orfalea, Richard Branson,
    Robert Woodruff, Sir Peter Leitch, Ted Turner, William Hewlett

Creators – Architects, Engineers, Inventors, Designers:
    Christopher Lowell, Henry Franks, James Lovelock, John Britten,
    Jørn Utzon, Ky Michealson, Paul MacCready, Thomas Edison,
    Tommy Hilfiger

Government & Politics:

Law & Justice:
    David Boies, Erin Brockovich, Jeffrey H. Gallet

Political and Military Leaders:
    Andrew Jackson, Dan Malloy, Erna Solberg, Gavin Newsom,
    George Patton, George Washington, King Carl XVI Gustaf,
    Nelson Rockefeller, Paul Wellstone, Woodrow Wilson

Performing Arts:

Actors:
    Billy Bob Thornton, Danny Glover, Harry Anderson,
    Henry Winkler, Jay Leno, Jennifer Aniston, Jim Carrey,
    Keanu Reeves, Kiera Knightley, Loretta Young, Octavia Spencer,
    Oliver Reed, Orlando Bloom, Susan Hampshire, Tom Smothers,
    Vince Vaughn, Whoopi Goldberg

Music and Dance:
Aakash Odedra, Annie Crummer, Bob Weir, Brad Little, Cher, Harry Belafonte, John Lennon, Nigel Kennedy

Science and Medicine:

Health Sciences:
Carol Greider, Fred Epstein, Harvey Cushing, Peter Lovatt

Research Scientists:
Albert Einstein, Ann Bancroft, Archer J.P. Martin, Jack Horner, Matthew H. Schneps, Michael Faraday, Pierre Curie

Visual Arts

Film & Photography
Ansel Adams, David Bailey, Nicole Betancourt, Robert Benton, Steven Spielberg, Søren KraghJacobsen, Walt Disney

Painting, Sculpting, Digital Arts
Andy Warhol, Auguste Rodin, Bennett Strahan, Chuck Close, Ian Marley, Ignacio Gomez, Leonardo da Vinci, Pablo Picasso, Robert Rauschenberg, Robert Toth, Willard Wigan

Writers:

Fiction Writers:
Agatha Christie, Elizabeth Daniels Squire, F. Scott Fitzgerald, Fannie Flagg, Gustave Flaubert, Jane Elson, John Corrigan, Natasha Solomons, Stephen Cannell, Terry Goodkind, Victor Villaseñor

Journalists:
Anja Dembina, Byron Pitts, Richard Engel, Scott Adams

Literature for Children and Young Adults:
Amber Lee Dodd, Avi, Hans Christian Andersen, Jeanne Betancourt, Patricia Polacco, Sally Gardner

Nonfiction:
Andrew Dornenburg, Bernie Taylor, Charley Boorman, Eileen Simpson, John Edmund Delezen, Larry Chambers, Nelson Lauver

Poets:
Philip Schultz, William Butler Yeats

"If you can't read well enough to function in this society, then you can't function in society. If they cannot read, you need to teach them. It doesn't matter what you call it, and it is the school's responsibility." *Dolores Howell*

www.ingramcontent.com/pod-product-compliance
Lightning Source LLC
Chambersburg PA
CBHW022009090426
42741CB00007B/953